Speak with Strength

The Art of Assertive Communication

Morgan Laine

Summary

Chapter 1: Understanding Assertive Communication

Effective communication is the cornerstone of human interaction. It is the bridge that connects us, helps us convey our thoughts and ideas, and enables us to understand others. However, not all forms of communication are equal. Some methods can be passive, leading to indifference or unassertiveness, while others may be aggressive, causing tension and conflict. In this chapter, we will explore the concept of assertive communication, its importance, and how it can enhance our personal and professional interactions.

Defining Assertive Communication

Assertive communication is an approach that allows individuals to express their thoughts, feelings, and opinions in a respectful and confident manner. Unlike passive communication, where one may avoid confrontation and fail to voice their needs, or aggressive communication, which involves forcing one's opinion upon others, assertive communication strikes a balance. It acknowledges both the rights of the communicator and the person or people they are communicating with. It seeks to express oneself clearly while demonstrating respect and empathy.

The Key Elements of Assertive Communication

To grasp the essence of assertive communication, we need to delve into its fundamental elements. These components provide a framework for understanding and practicing this communication style effectively.

1. Open and Honest Expression: Assertive communication encourages individuals to express themselves openly and truthfully. It entails sharing ideas, concerns, or emotions without fear of judgment or retribution. By creating an open dialogue, assertive communicators foster trust, enhance understanding, and promote healthy relationships.

2. Active Listening: Listening attentively is equally crucial in assertive communication. It involves offering our undivided attention, focusing on the speaker's verbal and nonverbal cues, and attempting to empathize with their perspective. Active listening allows for a better understanding of the message being conveyed and lays the foundation for a meaningful exchange of ideas.

3. Body Language and Vocal Tone: Nonverbal cues play a significant role in assertive communication. Maintaining an upright posture, making appropriate eye contact, and having a relaxed yet confident demeanor can enhance the impact of our message. Similarly, the tone of our voice can convey our intentions and emotions. A calm and

assertive vocal tone promotes understanding and facilitates a productive conversation.

4. Saying "No" Respectfully: Being able to say "no" is an essential aspect of assertive communication. Many individuals struggle with declining requests or setting boundaries for fear of disappointing or offending others. Assertive communicators, however, understand that saying "no" is not only their right but also a means of self-care and self-respect. They express their refusal respectfully, while considering the needs of others, and offer alternative solutions if possible.

The Benefits of Assertive Communication

Adopting an assertive communication style can yield an array of benefits in our personal and professional lives. Let us explore some of these advantages:

1. Building Better Relationships: Assertive communication fosters effective and meaningful relationships. By expressing ourselves honestly and respectfully, we create an environment of trust and understanding. It allows others to feel valued and encourages them to reciprocate, leading to stronger connections.

2. Conflict Resolution: Conflict is an inevitable part of human interaction. However, assertive communicators are skilled at

managing conflicts constructively. They can articulate their concerns and perspectives in a composed manner while actively listening to opposing viewpoints. This open dialogue paves the way for effective conflict resolution and mutual understanding.

3. Increased Self-Confidence: Practicing assertive communication enhances self-confidence. By asserting our needs and opinions, we learn to trust our own judgment and develop a sense of self-worth. This increased confidence has a positive ripple effect in all areas of life, empowering us to pursue our goals, make decisions, and stand up for ourselves.

4. Effective Negotiation: Assertive communicators excel at negotiation. By clearly conveying their interests, they can work towards finding mutually satisfactory solutions. The ability to communicate assertively during negotiations can lead to successful outcomes, whether in the workplace or personal relationships.

5. Reduced Stress and Anxiety: Passive or aggressive communication often results in heightened stress levels and increased anxiety. By adopting an assertive approach, individuals can effectively express their needs and boundaries, reducing stress and promoting emotional well-being.

Developing Your Assertive Communication Skills

Becoming an assertive communicator is a process that requires practice, self-reflection, and dedication. Here are some strategies to develop and enhance your assertive communication skills:

1. Self-Awareness: Begin by reflecting on your current communication style. Identify moments when you may have exhibited passive or aggressive behavior and consider the impact it had on yourself and others. Developing self-awareness is crucial for making positive changes.

2. Practice Active Listening: Make a conscious effort to actively listen when engaging in conversations. This means setting aside distractions, providing your undivided attention, and genuinely seeking to understand the speaker's perspective and underlying emotions.

3. Use "I" Statements: When expressing your thoughts or concerns, use "I" statements instead of putting blame on others. For example, saying "I feel overwhelmed by the workload" rather than "You are assigning me too many tasks" fosters open dialogue and prevents defensiveness.

4. Set Boundaries: Recognize your limits and communicate them effectively. Practice saying "no" when necessary while suggesting alternative solutions or compromises. By setting and maintaining healthy boundaries, you will foster respect from others and preserve

your overall well-being.

5. Seek Feedback: Regularly seek feedback from trusted individuals to gain insight into how you communicate and understand areas that require improvement. Constructive criticism and guidance can help refine your assertive communication skills.

Assertive communication is a powerful tool that enables individuals to express themselves effectively, build meaningful relationships, and resolve conflicts constructively. By understanding its key elements and practicing the associated skills, we can enhance our personal and professional interactions. Remember, becoming assertive is not about dominating or silencing others; it is about finding our voice, listening to others, and fostering understanding.

Defining Communication Styles

In today's interconnected world, effective communication has become a crucial skill in both personal and professional relationships. Whether it be in a boardroom, a classroom, or even over a cup of coffee with a close friend, the way we communicate shapes our relationships and influences our ability to convey our thoughts and emotions effectively.

Communication styles vary greatly from one individual to another, influenced by a multitude of factors such as culture, upbringing, and personality. Understanding these diverse communication styles is key to building strong connections, resolving conflicts, and ultimately achieving successful outcomes in our interactions.

In this chapter, we will delve into the fascinating realm of communication styles, exploring their various dimensions, identifying common types, and discussing their respective strengths and weaknesses.

1.1 The Nature of Communication Styles

Communication styles refer to the unique ways in which individuals express themselves, receive information, and interpret messages. They encompass a broad range of characteristics that can be observed through verbal and non-verbal cues, including tone of voice, body language, use of words, level of assertiveness, and preference for specific communication channels.

It is important to note that communication styles are not inherently good or bad; rather, they are simply different ways of approaching and engaging in communication. Understanding these differences allows us to adapt our own style and respond effectively to others, fostering mutual understanding and respect.

1.2 Dimensions of Communication Styles

To better understand communication styles, it is essential to dive into the key dimensions that influence how individuals engage with others. These dimensions help us identify the unique patterns and preferences in how people communicate.

1.2.1 Direct versus Indirect Communication

One critical dimension of communication styles is the degree of directness or indirectness in expressing thoughts and emotions. Some individuals prefer a direct approach, communicating their ideas and feelings openly and explicitly. They value clarity, efficiency, and are often seen as assertive communicators.

On the other hand, individuals with an indirect communication style tend to convey their thoughts and emotions subtly, employing hints, non-verbal cues, or relying on context to convey their intended meaning. They may prioritize preserving harmony, avoiding confrontation, and valuing the overall atmosphere of the communication.

It's important to recognize and respect both direct and indirect communication styles, as each can be effective in different contexts. Misunderstanding can arise when individuals with different styles fail to recognize the nuances and expectations associated with each approach.

1.2.2 Formal versus Informal Communication

Another dimension that influences communication styles is the degree of formality or informality individuals employ in their interactions. Formal communication involves adherence to established rules, protocols, and etiquette. It emphasizes appropriate language, professional tone, and a structured approach. Individuals adopting a formal communication style are often seen as respectful, professional, and diplomatic.

Conversely, informal communication is more casual, relaxed, and spontaneous. It may involve the use of colloquial language, personal anecdotes, jokes, and informal gestures to establish a sense of rapport and friendliness. Informal communicators are often perceived as approachable, friendly, and personable.

Both formal and informal communication styles have their place in various situations, and being aware of the expectations within a given context is essential to communicate effectively.

1.2.3 Emotional Expression

The way emotions are expressed also shapes an individual's communication style. While some individuals openly express their emotions, wearing their heart on their sleeves, others prefer to keep their emotions private, displaying a more reserved demeanor.

Emotionally expressive communicators often use facial expressions, hand gestures, and varying intonation to convey their thoughts and emotions. They may be animated and passionate in their delivery, but this can also create challenges in managing their emotions during heated or tense conversations.

On the other hand, individuals with a more emotionally reserved style tend to maintain a calm and composed façade, masking their emotions. They may value rationality, logical reasoning, and consider emotional expression as a potential distraction or hindrance to effective communication.

Understanding and recognizing the emotional expression of others can help us adapt our own communication to establish empathy and create a supportive environment during interactions.

1.3 Common Communication Styles

While every individual has a unique communication style shaped by various factors, certain patterns and commonalities can be observed across individuals. Recognizing these common communication styles can provide valuable insights into how people prefer to communicate, enabling us to adjust our approach to foster positive and productive interactions.

1.3.1 The Analytical Style

The Analytical style of communication is characterized by logical reasoning, thorough analysis, and a preference for precise and accurate information. Individuals with this communication style tend to be methodical, data-driven, and objective in their approach. They prioritize facts and figures, relying on evidence to support their arguments.

Analytical communicators may take more time to process and organize their thoughts before sharing them. They excel in presenting their ideas in a clear, concise, and detailed manner. However, they might be perceived as overly critical or detached due to their emphasis on facts over emotions.

1.3.2 The Assertive Style

Assertive communication is characterized by directness, confidence, and assertiveness in expressing thoughts and emotions. Individuals with this style prioritize clarity and transparency, openly stating their needs, opinions, and boundaries. They value clear communication and sharing their perspectives candidly.

Assertive communicators are active listeners, asking questions and seeking clarification when needed. They are comfortable with disagreement and often engage in constructive discussions. However, their directness can sometimes be intimidating or perceived as aggressive by others.

1.3.3 The Diplomatic Style

The Diplomatic communication style emphasizes harmony, respect, and preserving relationships. Individuals with this style prioritize maintaining a positive atmosphere, avoiding conflicts, and seeking common ground. They understand the importance of empathy and active listening in building rapport.

Diplomatic communicators often choose their words carefully, aiming to soften criticism and communicate sensitively. They value compromise and consensus-building and excel in diffusing tense situations. However, they may be perceived as indecisive or avoiding

confrontation due to their preference for consensus over
assertiveness.

1.3.4 The Expressive Style

Expressive communication is characterized by enthusiasm, energy,
and a preference for personal anecdotes and stories. Individuals with
this style tend to be animated, using a variety of gestures, facial
expressions, and varying tones to convey their ideas and emotions
effectively. They excel in building connections with others through
empathy and emotional resonance.

Expressive communicators are skilled at capturing attention, using
vivid language, and engaging their audience. However, their
tendency to focus on emotions rather than facts may be perceived as
less credible in certain professional settings. Additionally, their
passionate delivery can sometimes overshadow their intended
message.

1.3.5 The Systematic Style

Systematic communication style emphasizes organization, structure,
and adherence to a predefined plan. Individuals with this style value
order, predictability, and consistency in their communication. They
strive to ensure everyone has a clear understanding of the steps,
deadlines, and expectations involved.

Systematic communicators are adept at breaking down complex information into manageable parts and providing a step-by-step approach. However, their inclination towards structure may hinder their adaptability in dynamic or unpredictable situations.

1.4 Communicating Across Styles

Understanding different communication styles is only the first step toward effective communication. Building strong relationships and achieving desired outcomes require the ability to communicate across styles, bridging gaps and adapting to the preferences and needs of others.

1.4.1 Flexibility and Adaptability

Flexibility and adaptability are key attributes in navigating diverse communication styles. It involves cultivating an awareness of our own style and preferences, as well as the ability to adjust our approach to accommodate others.

By recognizing the strengths and weaknesses of various communication styles, we can assess the needs of the situation and adjust our communication accordingly. Adapting our style can involve using a different tone, employing appropriate body language, or matching the level of formality preferred by others.

1.4.2 Active Listening and Empathy

Active listening and empathy form the foundation for effective communication across styles. Active listening involves fully focusing on the speaker, seeking to understand their message, and demonstrating investment in the conversation. Empathy, on the other hand, involves understanding and sharing the emotions and perspectives of others.

Practicing active listening and empathy enables us to acknowledge and validate different communication styles. By demonstrating genuine interest, paraphrasing, and reflecting on the speaker's emotions, we can foster a sense of understanding and rapport.

1.4.3 Clarification and Confirmation

To prevent misunderstandings that may arise from different communication styles, clarification and confirmation are crucial. It involves restating or paraphrasing the message to ensure accurate understanding and seeking confirmation from the speaker. Asking clarifying questions can help unearth any underlying assumptions or unexpressed needs, ensuring that the intended message is received correctly. Additionally, summarizing the conversation at the end can help identify any potential areas of disagreement or misunderstanding, providing an opportunity for timely resolution.

The Importance of Assertiveness

In our journey through life, we often find ourselves faced with various situations where we need to communicate our needs, opinions, and boundaries. The ability to express ourselves effectively and assertively is a crucial skill that can have a profound impact on our personal and professional lives. In this chapter, we will explore the importance of assertiveness, its benefits, and how it can empower us to navigate life's challenges with confidence and authenticity.

Understanding Assertiveness:

Assertiveness is a communication style characterized by expressing our thoughts, feelings, and needs in a clear, direct, and respectful manner. It involves advocating for oneself while also considering the rights and feelings of others. Unlike aggression or passive behavior, assertiveness strikes a balance between these two extremes and allows individuals to assert their rights without infringing on the rights of others.

Assertiveness in Personal Relationships:

Developing assertiveness skills is particularly vital in personal relationships. Whether it is with family, friends, or romantic partners, assertiveness fosters healthy boundaries, effective conflict resolution, and enhances overall relationship satisfaction. When we are assertive, we communicate our needs and expectations openly, leading to a greater understanding between individuals.

For example, let's consider a scenario where a person constantly feels overwhelmed because their friend consistently asks them to do favors without reciprocating. By practicing assertiveness, they can express how they feel and establish boundaries to ensure a more balanced and fulfilling friendship. This ability to express oneself honestly can strengthen relationships and prevent resentment from building up.

Assertiveness in the Workplace:

Assertiveness is equally important in the professional realm. In the workplace, assertive individuals can confidently share their ideas, negotiate for fair treatment, and assert their rights without fear of being taken advantage of. This skill enhances productivity, empowers employees, and contributes to a healthy work environment.

Leaders who exhibit assertiveness inspire their team members, providing clarity in goals, expectations, and directions. They encourage open communication, value diverse viewpoints, and promote accountability. Organizations that foster an assertive culture benefit from increased team collaboration, better decision-making processes, and overall employee satisfaction.

The Benefits of Assertiveness:

1. Self-Confidence: Assertiveness fosters self-assurance and a positive self-image. When we can comfortably express ourselves and stand up for our beliefs, we develop confidence in our abilities and opinions.

2. Improved Communication: Assertiveness allows for clear and effective communication. By expressing ourselves honestly and respectfully, we increase the likelihood of being heard, understood, and taken seriously.

3. Enhanced Self-Esteem: When we advocate for ourselves and our needs, we reinforce a healthy sense of self-worth. Assertiveness prevents us from sacrificing our own happiness and well-being for the sake of others.

4. Reduced Resentment: By communicating assertively, we prevent unresolved issues from festering, which can lead to resentment and feelings of unmet expectations. Addressing concerns directly avoids conflict escalation and builds healthier relationships.

5. Boundaries and Respect: Assertiveness helps establish and maintain healthy boundaries. When we communicate our limits and expectations concisely, we enable others to respect our needs and autonomy, fostering mutual understanding and respect.

6. Conflict Resolution: Assertive individuals excel in conflict resolution. By honestly expressing their concerns and actively listening, they set the stage for productive and respectful discussions, leading to mutually beneficial outcomes.

Developing Assertiveness Skills:

While some individuals may naturally possess assertiveness skills, for most of us, it requires practice and conscious effort. Here are some techniques to develop assertiveness:

1. Self-awareness: Understand your needs, values, and boundaries. Reflect on your feelings and identify situations where you need to be more assertive.

2. Active Listening: Listening attentively to others' perspectives helps cultivate empathy and understanding. Recognizing others' viewpoints often makes it easier to advocate for your own needs while considering theirs simultaneously.

3. "I" Statements: Start sentences with phrases like "I feel" or "I

need" to express your emotions and requirements. This emphasizes personal responsibility and helps avoid blaming or accusing others.

4. Assertive Body Language: Stand tall, maintain eye contact, and speak clearly and confidently. Nonverbal cues play a significant role in conveying assertiveness and ensuring your message is received as intended.

5. Practice Assertive Responses: Role-play various scenarios where assertiveness is required. Practice using assertive language and responding to potential objections or pushback.

6. Recognize and Celebrate Progress: As you develop your assertiveness skills, celebrate your successes. Acknowledge the areas where you have become more assertive, and take note of the positive outcomes it brings.

Assertiveness is an invaluable skill that empowers individuals to effectively express themselves, establish healthy boundaries, and build harmonious relationships both personally and professionally. It is a key ingredient for self-confidence, improved communication, and conflict resolution. By nurturing assertiveness, we can navigate life's challenges with authenticity, integrity, and a sense of empowerment.

Common Misconceptions

Assertiveness is an important communication and interpersonal skill that involves expressing your thoughts, feelings, and needs in a clear and confident manner while respecting the rights and opinions of others. However, there are several misconceptions about assertiveness that can lead to misunderstandings or ineffective communication. Here are some common misconceptions:

Aggressiveness is the same as assertiveness: One of the most prevalent misconceptions is that assertiveness is the same as aggressiveness. Aggressiveness involves pushing one's own needs and opinions at the expense of others, often in a confrontational and disrespectful manner. Assertiveness, on the other hand, aims to express oneself honestly while still considering the feelings and viewpoints of others.

Being assertive means always saying "yes": Some people believe that being assertive means always agreeing to others' requests and never saying no. However, assertiveness involves expressing your needs and limits, which sometimes means saying no or setting boundaries when necessary. It's about finding a balance between accommodating others and taking care of your own well-being.

Assertiveness is rude or selfish: Some individuals fear that being assertive might come across as rude or selfish. However, assertiveness is about clear communication and expressing your thoughts and feelings respectfully. It doesn't entail disregarding others; rather, it promotes open dialogue and understanding.

It's about getting your way: Assertiveness is often mistaken for trying to control situations to get what you want. While it does involve expressing your needs and desires, it also involves active listening and finding mutually beneficial solutions. It's not about dominating others, but rather about finding common ground.

Always maintaining a strong demeanor: Another misconception is that assertive individuals must always display a strong and confident demeanor. In reality, assertiveness can be expressed calmly and without aggression. It's more about effectively conveying your message than showing dominance.

It's an inborn trait: Many people believe that assertiveness is something you're either born with or without. In reality, assertiveness is a skill that can be learned and developed over time through practice and self-awareness. Anyone can work on becoming more assertive.

Avoiding conflict means being assertive: Some individuals think that avoiding conflict is the same as being assertive. While assertiveness can help prevent unnecessary conflicts, it doesn't mean completely avoiding difficult conversations. Assertiveness involves addressing issues openly and honestly, which can lead to better understanding and resolution.

It's about speaking more: Being assertive isn't solely about speaking up; it also involves active listening and valuing others' perspectives. Engaging in meaningful dialogue and understanding others' viewpoints is just as important as expressing your own.

In summary, assertiveness is a balanced communication skill that involves expressing oneself clearly, respectfully, and honestly while considering the feelings and viewpoints of others. It's not about aggression, dominance, or always getting your way, but rather about effective and empathetic communication.

Benefits in Personal and Professional Life

In this chapter, we will delve into the myriad of benefits that an individual can derive from focusing on personal and professional development. While personal and professional lives may seemingly exist in separate realms, they are deeply intertwined, and growth in one can positively impact the other. Developing oneself holistically can lead to a more balanced and fulfilling life, propelling both personal happiness and professional success. In this chapter, we will explore the ways in which personal and professional development intersect, creating a virtuous cycle of growth, and we will discuss some practical strategies for achieving harmony in these two important aspects of our lives.

Section 1: Personal Growth and its Impact on Professional Life

1.1 Increased Self-Awareness:

One of the key benefits of personal growth is the development of self-awareness. Understanding our own strengths, weaknesses, values, and motivations helps us make better decisions, set meaningful goals, and align our personal and professional lives. Self-awareness enables individuals to recognize their passions and interests, thereby guiding them towards career paths that resonate with their authentic selves. Moreover, a strong sense of self-awareness allows professionals to effectively navigate workplace dynamics, build strong relationships, and communicate more effectively with colleagues and superiors.

1.2 Enhanced Emotional Intelligence:

Personal development often entails the cultivation of emotional intelligence, which serves as a valuable asset in the professional world. Emotional intelligence encompasses the ability to recognize and manage one's emotions, understand others' perspectives, and empathize with their experiences. Professionals with high emotional intelligence are better equipped to handle stress, resolve conflicts, and foster healthy work environments. They excel at building rapport with clients, negotiating, networking, and leading teams effectively. The cultivation of emotional intelligence through personal growth positively impacts overall job satisfaction and career advancement.

1.3 Improved Work-Life Balance:

By focusing on personal growth, individuals can better manage the delicate balance between work and personal life. Striking this balance is essential for maintaining mental well-being, preventing burnout, and nurturing relationships outside of work. When personal development involves building healthy habits, setting boundaries, and prioritizing self-care, professionals are more likely to be productive, engaged, and satisfied in their careers. Additionally, a harmonious work-life balance enables individuals to invest time and energy in personal passions and relationships, promoting personal happiness and fulfillment.

Section 2: Professional Growth and its Implications on Personal Life

2.1 Enhanced Skill Set:

Professional growth often entails acquiring new skills, advancing existing ones, and staying abreast of industry trends. This continuous learning process not only contributes to career advancement but also spills over into personal life. Developing new skills can lead to increased confidence, expanded perspectives, and opportunities for personal expression. Skills such as effective communication, leadership, and problem-solving are invaluable not only in the workplace but also in personal relationships and endeavors.

2.2 Expanded Network:

Through professional development efforts such as attending conferences, workshops, or joining industry associations, individuals have the opportunity to expand their professional networks. These connections not only provide access to new career opportunities but also broaden one's personal network. Cultivating diverse connections can introduce individuals to new ideas, perspectives, and cultural experiences that enrich personal life. It fosters the formation of supportive friendships and offers opportunities for collaboration, personal growth, and shared recreational pursuits.

2.3 Increased Confidence and Personal Fulfilment:

Setting and achieving professional goals can enhance an individual's self-confidence, self-worth, and overall personal fulfillment. Progressing in one's career, overcoming challenges, and witnessing personal growth breeds a sense of accomplishment that positively impacts all areas of life. A fulfilling professional life contributes to a greater sense of satisfaction, happiness, and overall well-being. The confidence gained through professional achievements often spills over into personal life, allowing individuals to pursue hobbies, relationships, and personal passions with renewed vigor and belief in their abilities.

Section 3: Strategies for Holistic Growth

3.1 Goal Setting and Planning:

To achieve holistic growth, individuals must set clear goals and develop action plans that encompass both personal and professional aspirations. By aligning these goals, individuals can ensure they complement and strengthen each other. It is essential to reflect on personal values, interests, and core beliefs while setting goals, ensuring they resonate with the individual's authentic self. Regularly reassessing and refining these goals guarantees a steady path towards growth, fulfillment, and the harmonization of personal and professional aspirations.

3.2 Continuous Learning:

Both personal and professional growth are deeply linked to continuous learning. Investing time and effort into acquiring new knowledge, skills, and perspectives is crucial for staying relevant, adaptable, and engaged. Taking up online courses, attending seminars, reading books, and seeking mentorship are effective ways to embark on a lifelong learning journey. Engaging in diverse learning experiences not only enhances professional competence but also stimulates personal growth and cultivates a well-rounded individual.

3.3 Embracing Challenges and Seeking Feedback:

Embracing challenges and seeking feedback are essential for personal and professional growth. Stepping out of one's comfort zone, taking on new responsibilities, and tackling difficult tasks fosters resilience, adaptability, and personal development.

Constructive feedback helps individuals identify areas for improvement, develop self-awareness, and refine their skills. By proactively seeking feedback, professionals can continuously enhance their performance and maintain a growth mindset that extends beyond the workplace.

3.4 Cultivating a Supportive Network:

Surrounding oneself with a supportive network is fundamental to holistic growth. Building relationships with mentors, colleagues, friends, and family members who encourage personal and professional development can provide invaluable guidance, motivation, and accountability. Investing time in nurturing these relationships fosters emotional well-being, loyalty, and mutual growth. A supportive network serves as a constant source of inspiration, challenging beliefs, offering guidance, and celebrating the milestones achieved on the path of personal and professional growth.

Chapter 2: Core Principles of Assertive Communication

In today's fast-paced and interconnected world, effective communication skills have become more crucial than ever. From personal relationships to professional settings, the ability to express ourselves assertively can greatly enhance our interactions and lead to more successful outcomes. In this chapter, we will delve into the core principles of assertive communication, exploring its benefits, techniques, and key components. By understanding and applying these principles, we can improve our communication skills and foster healthier and more productive relationships.

Understanding Assertiveness

Assertiveness is often misunderstood or confused with aggressiveness or passivity. However, it is important to differentiate between these three communication styles. Assertiveness involves expressing one's thoughts, feelings, and needs in a clear, honest, and respectful manner while simultaneously respecting the rights and opinions of others. It is a balanced approach that values open and direct communication, leading to better understanding and problem-solving.

Benefits of Assertive Communication

Practicing assertive communication offers numerous benefits in various aspects of life. Firstly, it helps build self-confidence and self-esteem. By expressing ourselves assertively, we convey our self-worth and value our own needs and opinions. This, in turn, contributes to a sense of empowerment and personal growth.

Secondly, assertive communication fosters strong and fulfilling relationships. When we communicate assertively, we establish clear boundaries, express appreciation and empathy towards others, and maintain open lines of dialogue. This builds a foundation of trust, respect, and understanding, enhancing the dynamics of our relationships.

Furthermore, assertiveness facilitates effective decision-making and conflict resolution. By expressing our thoughts and concerns openly and honestly, we create an environment where problems can be addressed collaboratively and solutions can be reached more easily.

Assertive Communication Techniques

To become more assertive communicators, there are several techniques we can practice and implement:

1. "I" Statements: Using "I" statements allows us to express our thoughts and feelings without blaming or accusing others. For example, instead of saying, "You never listen to me," we can rephrase it as "I feel unheard when I try to share my thoughts with you." This approach emphasizes personal experiences rather than criticizing or attacking others.

2. Active Listening: An essential aspect of effective communication is active listening. It involves fully engaging with the speaker, maintaining eye contact, nodding, and summarizing what has been said to ensure understanding. Active listening demonstrates respect and fosters a deeper connection during conversations.

3. Setting Boundaries: Assertiveness requires the ability to set and communicate clear boundaries. It is important to know our limits and communicate them assertively when necessary. By doing so, we prevent others from taking advantage of us and ensure our own well-being.

4. Empathy and Understanding: Being empathetic towards others' perspectives and feelings is crucial in assertive communication. Genuine understanding and acknowledgment of others' opinions, emotions, and experiences can be instrumental in resolving conflicts and fostering healthy relationships.

Key Components of Assertive Communication

While there are various components of assertive communication, a few key elements lay the foundation for its success:

1. Tone of Voice and Body Language: The way we speak and present

ourselves greatly impacts how others perceive us. Assertive communication involves maintaining a calm and confident tone of voice, avoiding aggression or passivity. Additionally, utilizing open body language such as maintaining eye contact and avoiding defensive postures enhances our message's clarity and authenticity.

2. Self-Respect and Respect for Others: Assertive communication includes respecting ourselves and others equally. This means acknowledging our own worth and the value of our own opinions while appreciating the perspectives and ideas of others. Mutual respect forms the basis for healthy and productive communication.

3. Openness to Feedback: Being open to receiving and giving feedback is essential in assertive communication. Constructive feedback allows us to grow, learn from our mistakes, and improve our communication skills. It is important to approach feedback with an open mind, free from defensiveness or judgment, in order to foster personal and professional growth.

Understanding and applying the core principles of assertive communication is a transformative skill that can positively impact all areas of our lives. By embracing this approach, we develop more authentic connections, enhance our self-confidence, and improve our problem-solving and decision-making abilities. Remember, assertive communication is not about dominance or control but rather creating an environment where everyone feels heard, respected, and valued. By practicing assertiveness in our daily interactions, we can cultivate stronger relationships and navigate conflicts more effectively, ultimately leading to a more fulfilling and successful life.

Clear and Direct Expression

In the vast realm of communication, clarity and directness serve as the vital pillars that uphold effective expression. Whether it be conveying your thoughts through written word or articulating ideas in spoken language, the ability to communicate clearly and directly can significantly impact the success of any endeavor. This chapter delves into the essence of clear and direct expression, examining its significance, essential elements, and strategies that can be employed to master this art form. Join us on this journey, as we explore the power of language and its capacity to transform mere words into compelling, resonant messages.

Section 2.1: The Significance of Clear and Direct Expression

Clear and direct expression stands as a cornerstone of effective communication, playing a pivotal role in various aspects of our lives. Whether it's in professional settings, personal relationships, or even within ourselves, the impact of clear and direct expression cannot be overstated. Let us delve deeper into its significance and explore the ways it can enhance our interactions.

1. Fostering Understanding

At its core, communication aims to convey ideas and exchange information, fostering understanding between individuals. Clear and direct expression serves as a catalyst for this understanding, cutting through the noise and ambiguity that can muddy our messages. By employing language that is concise, transparent, and unambiguous, we can ensure that our ideas are grasped accurately, promoting effective exchange and reducing potential misunderstanding or misinterpretation.

Consider a professional setting, where clear communication is paramount. Suppose a project manager seeks to convey the goals, objectives, and timelines to their team. A clear and direct expression ensures that everyone is on the same page, minimizing the chance of miscommunication that could result in misguided efforts or missed deadlines.

2. Building Trust and Rapport

Effective communication is not solely about exchanging information; it also fosters trust, rapport, and meaningful connections between individuals. Clear and direct expression cultivates an environment of transparency and honesty, establishing a strong foundation for trust to flourish. When individuals express themselves openly and sincerely, their intentions are laid bare, leaving no room for doubt or skepticism. This sincerity nurtures a safe and authentic space for meaningful conversations, fostering stronger relationships, and building lasting bonds.

3. Enhancing Persuasion and Influence

Communication, particularly in persuasive contexts, hinges on the ability to capture attention, engage the audience, and motivate them to action. Clear and direct expression plays a crucial role in achieving this objective. When messages are presented in a concise, straightforward manner, they resonate more powerfully with the intended audience, leaving a lasting impact. By stripping away unnecessary complexities and delivering a clear, well-articulated argument, communicators can effectively persuade and influence their listeners or readers.

Mastering Clear and Direct Expression

Clear and direct expression is not an inherent skill but rather a craft that can be honed through conscious effort and practice. This section outlines several essential elements and strategies that can aid individuals in mastering this art form.

1. Simplicity in Language

The first step towards achieving clarity and directness in expression is simplifying language. Use straightforward, everyday language that is easily understood by a wide range of audiences. Avoid jargon, complex terminology, or convoluted phrases that may confuse or alienate the recipients of your message. Remember, effective communication does not require a display of linguistic prowess but rather the ability to convey ideas in a manner that is straightforward and accessible.

2. Organization and Structure

Thoughtful organization and structure are vital components of clear and direct expression. Begin by outlining the main points or ideas you wish to convey, ensuring a logical flow. Present information in a coherent manner, using headings, bullet points, or numbered lists to enhance readability. By organizing your thoughts effectively, you facilitate understanding and enable your audience to follow along effortlessly.

3. Clarity through Conciseness

Conciseness is the hallmark of clear and direct expression. Aim to convey your message concisely, without sacrificing essential information. Avoid excessive use of adjectives, adverbs, or unnecessary details that can dilute your primary message. Instead, select words carefully, omit redundancies, and strive for precision. When ideas are presented succinctly, they have a more significant impact on the recipients and are more likely to be remembered.

4. Active Voice

Utilizing the active voice leads to clearer, more direct expression. Passive voice can obscure the doer of the action and dilute the impact of the message. By using the active voice, the subject becomes the protagonist of the sentence, enhancing clarity and directness. For example, the sentence "The team completed the project successfully" is more direct and impactful than "The project was completed successfully by the team."

5. Verbal and Non-Verbal Cues

While clear and direct expression is commonly associated with written communication, it also plays a vital role in verbal exchanges. Pay close attention to your tone of voice, body language, and facial expressions to ensure congruence with your spoken words. Maintaining eye contact, using appropriate gestures, and modulating your tone can amplify the clarity and directness of your message, making it more impactful and leaving a lasting impression on your audience.

Clear and direct expression, the hallmark of effective communication, is an art form that can significantly influence our personal and professional lives. By fostering understanding, building trust and rapport, and enhancing persuasion and influence, it sets the stage for meaningful connections and successful outcomes. With the essential elements and strategies outlined in this chapter, individuals can embark on a journey towards mastering this art form, enriching their communication skills, and transforming mere words into powerful, resonant messages.

Respectful Listening

In today's fast-paced world, where everyone is constantly rushing from one place to another, meaningful communication has become a rare commodity. We are so consumed with our own thoughts and opinions that we often forget to truly listen to others. But what if I were to tell you that by honing the art of respectful listening, we can not only strengthen our relationships but also open ourselves up to new perspectives and ideas?

In this chapter, we will delve deep into the concept of respectful listening – a skill that goes far beyond hearing words but truly understanding and valuing the speaker's thoughts and emotions. Through practical tips and valuable insights, we will explore how to become a masterful respectful listener, capable of fostering meaningful connections and nurturing personal growth.

Section 1: Understanding Respectful Listening

1.1 The Difference between Hearing and Listening

When we hear, we merely absorb sound waves without making a conscious effort to understand the message being conveyed. Listening, on the other hand, involves actively engaging with the speaker's words, seeking to comprehend their message, and empathizing with their emotions. Respectful listening transcends the surface level, demonstrating genuine interest and respect for the speaker.

1.2 The Importance of Respectful Listening

Listening respectfully has far-reaching benefits that extend beyond the immediate interaction. It strengthens relationships by making others feel valued and understood. It opens doors to personal growth by exposing us to diverse perspectives and opportunities for learning. Respectful listening also promotes a cooperative and inclusive environment, enabling collaborative problem-solving and fostering creativity.

Section 2: Becoming a Respectful Listener

2.1 Cultivating Empathy

One of the fundamental pillars of respectful listening is empathy. It involves seeing the world through the speaker's eyes, understanding their emotions, and recognizing their experiences as valid. Empathy enables us to connect with others on a deeper level, creating a safe space for them to express themselves freely.

2.2 Active Listening

Active listening is a powerful tool that can transform our communication skills. By giving our undivided attention, maintaining eye contact, and providing verbal or non-verbal cues of comprehension, we communicate our genuine interest in what the speaker has to say. Active listening also involves asking open-ended questions, seeking clarification, and summarizing key points to display our engagement and understanding.

2.3 Overcoming Biases and Assumptions

Our biases and assumptions can hinder our ability to listen respectfully. Preconceived notions prevent us from truly hearing and understanding the speaker's perspective. By consciously acknowledging and challenging our biases, we can create an open and non-judgmental space where others feel safe expressing themselves.

Section 3: Enhancing Respectful Listening Skills

3.1 Mindfulness and Presence

Practicing mindfulness and being fully present in the moment is essential for respectful listening. It involves letting go of distractions, both internal and external, and focusing on the speaker's words and emotions. Developing this skill requires patience, self-awareness, and a commitment to giving our attention wholeheartedly.

3.2 Suspending Judgment

Respectful listening requires suspending judgment and holding space for diverse opinions and experiences. While it is natural to have different perspectives, it is crucial to approach conversations with an open mind and genuine curiosity. By embracing the unknown, we foster an atmosphere of acceptance and create opportunities for growth and learning.

Section 4: Applying Respectful Listening in Various Settings

4.1 Personal Relationships

Respectful listening serves as the cornerstone of healthy personal relationships. By making an effort to understand and empathize with our loved ones, we strengthen the bond, enhance trust, and foster a sense of mutual respect. In the context of conflicts, respectful listening facilitates effective communication and paves the way for resolution and understanding.

4.2 Workplace Communication

In the professional realm, respectful listening plays a vital role in fostering teamwork, increasing productivity, and promoting innovation. By valuing diverse ideas, actively seeking input from all team members, and engaging in meaningful dialogue, organizations can build a culture of collaboration and inclusivity.

4.3 Public Speaking and Presentations

For public speakers, respectful listening goes beyond being a skill possessed by the audience. It involves understanding the audience's needs, adapting the message accordingly, and utilizing effective listening techniques to connect on a deeper level. By fostering a sense of respect and trust, public speakers can captivate their audience and deliver impactful presentations.

Respectful listening is an art that requires continuous practice, patience, and self-reflection. By prioritizing understanding, empathy, and open-mindedness, we can unlock the transformative power of communication. Whether in personal relationships, professional settings, or public speaking, the ability to truly listen and appreciate others' voices is a gateway to growth, connection, and a more compassionate world.

So, let us embark on this journey together, embracing the power of respectful listening, and watch as our relationships flourish, our horizons expand, and our own lives become enriched by the wisdom and experiences of others.

Self-Awareness and Emotional Regulation

In the fascinating journey of self-discovery and personal growth, self-awareness and emotional regulation hold pivotal roles. These two interconnected concepts provide us with invaluable insights into our thoughts, feelings, and behaviors, enabling us to navigate life's challenges with grace and resilience. This chapter explores the profound significance of self-awareness and emotional regulation, delving into their intricacies and explaining how they contribute to our overall well-being.

Understanding Self-Awareness:

Self-awareness is the foundation of personal growth and the key to understanding ourselves at a deeper level. It involves being cognizant of our emotions, strengths, weaknesses, beliefs, and values. By developing self-awareness, we gain a clearer understanding of why we behave in certain ways and how our actions impact ourselves and those around us.

To cultivate self-awareness, it is essential to engage in self-reflection. This practice involves setting aside time to introspect and evaluate our thoughts, emotions, and behaviors without judgment. By becoming aware of our inner dialogue, we can identify negative self-talk patterns and transform them into positive and empowering thoughts.

Additionally, self-awareness can be enhanced through mindfulness, a practice that involves being fully present in the moment. Mindfulness allows us to observe our thoughts and emotions without becoming entangled in them. By developing this skill, we can detach ourselves from stressful situations and respond in a more composed and thoughtful manner.

The Link between Self-Awareness and Emotional Regulation:

Self-awareness and emotional regulation are intimately linked, as one cannot be effectively achieved without the other. Emotional regulation refers to the ability to manage and control our emotions in a healthy and adaptive manner. It entails understanding our emotional triggers, recognizing the physiological and cognitive aspects of our emotional responses, and choosing appropriate strategies to regulate our emotions.

Self-awareness provides us with the necessary insights to recognize and understand our emotions. By being aware of the emotions we are experiencing, we can take proactive steps to regulate them effectively. For instance, if we notice that we often feel anxious in certain situations, being self-aware allows us to identify the underlying causes of our anxiety, such as fear or self-doubt. Armed with this knowledge, we can then employ appropriate techniques, such as deep breathing or positive affirmations, to regulate our anxiety.

Importance of Emotional Regulation:

Emotional regulation is a vital skill that contributes to our overall well-being and interpersonal relationships. Research has demonstrated that individuals who possess effective emotional regulation strategies experience lower levels of stress, better mental health, and improved overall life satisfaction.

One of the key benefits of emotional regulation is its impact on our relationships. When we can regulate our emotions, we are less likely to react impulsively or lash out in anger, which can strain relationships and create conflicts. Instead, we can respond mindfully, considering the emotions of others and expressing ourselves in a calm and constructive manner.

Moreover, emotional regulation empowers us to navigate life's challenges with resilience. By managing our emotions effectively, we can remain focused and goal-oriented, even in the face of adversity. This skill enables us to bounce back from setbacks, cope with stress more effectively, and maintain a positive outlook on life.

Developing Emotional Regulation Skills:

Developing emotional regulation skills requires practice and dedication. Here are some effective strategies to enhance emotional regulation:

1. Self-reflection: Engage in regular self-reflection to identify your emotional triggers and patterns. This self-awareness will enable you to anticipate and manage your emotions more effectively.

2. Mindfulness: Practice mindfulness meditation to cultivate present-moment awareness and enhance your ability to observe and regulate your emotions without judgment.

3. Cognitive restructuring: Challenge and reframe negative thought patterns that contribute to emotional distress. Replace irrational thoughts with realistic and positive beliefs that promote emotional well-being.

4. Emotional awareness exercises: Engage in activities that enhance emotional awareness, such as journaling, keeping an emotion log, or discussing emotions with a trusted friend or therapist.

5. Relaxation techniques: Learn and practice relaxation techniques like deep breathing, progressive muscle relaxation, or visualization, as these can help reduce stress and promote emotional balance.

6. Seek support: Reach out to friends, family, or professionals for support and guidance when navigating challenging emotions or situations. Sometimes, seeking help can provide new perspectives and strategies for emotional regulation.

In the journey of self-discovery and personal growth, self-awareness and emotional regulation serve as powerful tools. By cultivating self-awareness, we gain deeper insights into our thoughts, emotions, and behaviors, facilitating personal growth and a better understanding of ourselves. Emotional regulation, on the other hand, equips us with the ability to manage and control our emotions in a healthy and adaptive manner. Together, these two concepts empower us to navigate life's challenges with resilience, maintain healthy relationships, and achieve a greater sense of well-being and fulfillment.

Confidence and Body Language

Confidence and body language are two interconnected aspects that play a significant role in our daily lives. Whether we realize it or not, the way we carry ourselves and the messages our bodies convey have a profound impact on how others perceive us. Moreover, our body language influences how we feel about ourselves and the level of confidence we exude. In this chapter, we will explore the intricate relationship between confidence and body language, delve into the nonverbal cues that signify confidence, and discuss practical strategies for improving both aspects in various contexts.

Understanding Confidence:

Confidence is a state of mind that reflects our belief in our abilities, skills, and worth. When we feel confident, we project an aura of self-assuredness and competence, which can be compelling and positively influence the way others perceive us. Conversely, a lack of confidence can make us appear unconvincing, timid, or uncertain.

Body Language and Confidence:

Body language, also known as nonverbal communication, encompasses the movements, gestures, and postures we adopt to express ourselves. It is often considered a more accurate indicator of our feelings and intentions than words alone. Our body language not only reflects our level of confidence but also has the potential to shape our internal state of mind. By consciously using positive body language, we can enhance our self-assurance and well-being.

Confidence-Building Body Language:

1. Posture:

One of the most prominent indicators of confidence is posture. Standing or sitting up straight demonstrates assurance and self-confidence. Conversely, slouching or hunching over can convey a lack of self-belief. Maintaining an open and upright posture not only signals confidence to others but also influences our own mental state, promoting positive feelings within ourselves.

2. Eye Contact:

Making and maintaining eye contact is a crucial element of confident body language. It conveys attentiveness, engagement, and trustworthiness. When we avoid eye contact, we may be perceived as lacking confidence or disinterested, thus undermining our ability to connect with others effectively. Practicing good eye contact demonstrates confidence and fosters better communication and rapport.

3. Hand Gestures:

Our hand gestures can significantly impact how others perceive us. Using purposeful and controlled hand movements while speaking enhances our ability to convey our message effectively. It exhibits confidence, enthusiasm, and conviction. However, overly fidgety or restricted hand movements can indicate nervousness or hesitation, diminishing the impact of our communication.

4. Facial Expressions:

Our facial expressions can convey a wealth of emotions and play a pivotal role in projecting confidence. A genuine smile, for example, can indicate approachability, friendliness, and confidence. Conversely, a tense or guarded facial expression can create barriers in interpersonal interactions. Being mindful of our facial expressions and ensuring they align with our intended message can greatly enhance our overall confidence and positive impact on others.

5. Voice Modulation:

The way we use our voice is another crucial aspect of confident body language. Speaking with clarity, volume, and emphasis projects confidence and allows others to perceive us as credible and knowledgeable. On the contrary, speaking too softly or timidly may undermine our presence and authority. Developing excellent vocal control and modulation amplifies our confidence in various situations, such as public speaking or leading a team.

Strategies for Building Confidence and Improving Body Language:

1. Practice Self-Awareness:

Developing self-awareness is fundamental to understanding and enhancing your body language and confidence. Pay close attention to your own postures, gestures, and expressions in different situations. Take note of any habits or tendencies that may indicate a lack of confidence and work towards replacing them with more positive, confident body language.

2. Visualize Success:

Visualization is a powerful tool to boost confidence. Before entering a challenging situation, try visualizing yourself acting confidently, using positive body language, and achieving a successful outcome. By mentally rehearsing confident behavior, you can program your mind to respond more confidently in real-life scenarios.

3. Enhance Posture and Body Awareness:

Engaging in activities like yoga, Pilates, or regular exercise can enhance both your posture and body awareness. These practices help develop core strength, improve posture, and increase mindfulness of your body positions and movements. By consciously practicing good posture and being aware of your body, you can project confidence effortlessly.

4. Seek Feedback:

To further develop your body language and confidence, seek feedback from trusted individuals or mentors. Ask them to observe your nonverbal cues and provide constructive criticism. This external perspective can shed light on areas for improvement that you may not have noticed on your own.

5. Embrace a Growth Mindset:

Adopting a growth mindset is crucial when working on confidence and body language. Understand that both aspects are flexible and can be improved with time, practice, and effort. Embrace challenges as opportunities to grow and learn, and be patient with yourself throughout the process.

Confidence and body language are intricately linked, influencing both how others perceive us and how we feel about ourselves. Through conscious awareness and practice, we can improve our body language, ultimately boosting our confidence and positively impacting our interactions with others. By incorporating the strategies outlined in this chapter, you can enhance your nonverbal communication, project confidence, and unlock your full potential in various personal and professional settings.

Chapter 3: Developing Assertiveness

In this chapter, we will delve into the empowering realm of assertiveness and explore its significance in our personal and professional lives. Assertiveness is a fundamental communication skill that allows us to express our wants, needs, and boundaries effectively while respecting the rights and opinions of others. By mastering assertiveness, we can enhance our self-confidence, improve our relationships, and overcome various challenges that life throws at us. So, let us embark on this transformative journey to develop assertiveness and unlock the full potential within ourselves.

Understanding Assertiveness:

Assertiveness is often misunderstood, mistaken for aggression or submission. However, it stands in its own distinct category, offering a balanced approach to communication. Unlike aggression, which involves imposing one's views upon others, and submission, which forfeits personal needs for the sake of others, assertiveness centers on open and honest expression while respecting the rights of all parties involved.

Assertiveness is not about winning or dominating conversations; instead, it focuses on fostering healthy dialogue, establishing clear boundaries, and advocating for ourselves. It allows us to take charge of our lives, build sturdy relationships, and develop a strong sense of self-worth.

The Benefits of Assertiveness:

Developing assertiveness has numerous benefits that extend beyond communication. When we embrace assertiveness in our lives, we stand to gain:

1. Enhanced Self-Confidence: Assertiveness empowers us to express our opinions and feelings confidently, leading to increased self-assurance and self-belief.

2. Improved Relationships: By clearly articulating our needs and boundaries, assertiveness fosters healthier and more respectful relationships. It enables effective conflict resolution and establishes better understanding between individuals.

3. Reduced Stress: Assertiveness helps us tackle stressful situations by allowing us to communicate our concerns openly and assert our rights. When we express our feelings and needs honestly, the burden of unspoken expectations and tension is reduced.

4. Personal Empowerment: Developing assertiveness equips us with the tools to make effective decisions, take charge of our lives, and pursue our goals without encroaching upon the rights of others.

Developing Assertiveness:

Now that we understand the importance of assertiveness, let's explore practical strategies to develop this invaluable communication skill:

1. Cultivate Self-Awareness: Begin by developing a deep understanding of your values, needs, and boundaries. Reflect on your emotions, thoughts, and beliefs, and become attuned to how they influence your communication style.

2. Practice Active Listening: Effective communication involves not only expressing our thoughts but also actively listening to others. Practice attentive listening by giving your full focus to the speaker, summarizing their main points, and asking clarifying questions.

3. Use "I" Statements: Frame your thoughts and feelings using "I" statements instead of accusing or attacking language. This approach allows for ownership of your emotions without placing blame on others. For example, say "I feel overwhelmed when the workload becomes unmanageable" instead of "You always overload me with work."

4. Set Clear Boundaries: Establishing boundaries is essential for maintaining healthy relationships. Be clear and direct when communicating your limits, ensuring that others understand and respect them. Remember, setting boundaries is not selfish; it is an act of self-preservation.

5. Practice Saying "No": Many people find it challenging to say "no" to requests, fearing disappointment or rejection. Learning to say "no" assertively and respectfully is crucial for maintaining balance and avoiding overcommitment. Practice declining requests while offering an alternative or explanation to ensure your response is understood.

6. Develop Assertive Body Language: Nonverbal cues play a vital role in communication, and our body language can convey assertiveness or submissiveness. Maintain eye contact, stand tall, use appropriate gestures, and speak with a clear and confident tone to reinforce your assertive message.

7. Embrace Constructive Feedback: Constructive feedback is an opportunity for growth and improvement. Learn to accept feedback gracefully by focusing on the message rather than becoming defensive. Seek clarification if needed, and express appreciation for the feedback received.

8. Practice Assertion in Various Settings: Start by practicing assertive communication in low-stakes scenarios, such as with friends or

family. Gradually apply assertiveness skills in more challenging situations, such as professional meetings or when addressing conflicts.

Mastering assertiveness is a lifelong journey that requires practice, self-reflection, and continuous growth. The benefits we gain from developing assertiveness extend far beyond effective communication. Assertiveness allows us to live authentically, honor our needs, and foster healthier relationships based on mutual respect and understanding. By committing to becoming more assertive, we can navigate life's challenges with confidence and achieve personal empowerment.

Cultivating Self-Confidence

Self-confidence is like a secret weapon that empowers individuals to take on life's challenges with grace and resilience. It is the ability to trust in your own abilities, worth, and judgment, allowing you to navigate through various situations effectively. Building and nurturing self-confidence is a lifelong journey that requires self-awareness, self-acceptance, and consistent practice. In this chapter, we will explore the importance of cultivating self-confidence, the barriers that hinder its growth, and practical strategies to enhance and maintain it.

Understanding the Significance of Self-Confidence

Self-confidence serves as a vital pillar of personal and professional success. It fuels ambition, determination, and a positive outlook. When you believe in yourself and your abilities, you are more likely to set ambitious goals and work tirelessly to achieve them. A confident person radiates an air of credibility and competence, fostering trust and respect from others. Furthermore, self-confidence frees us from the shackles of self-doubt, enabling us to embrace risks and learn from failures.

Barriers to Self-Confidence

Before we delve into nurturing self-confidence, it is essential to address the common barriers that can impede its growth. By recognizing and understanding these obstacles, we can develop effective strategies to overcome them.

1. Self-doubt and Negative Self-Talk: A negative internal dialogue can plague even the most talented individuals. Constantly questioning your abilities and worth undermines your self-confidence. It is crucial to become aware of this negative self-talk and replace it with positive affirmations and constructive thoughts.

2. Past Failures and Rejection: Previous setbacks and disappointments can leave deep emotional scars that linger. The fear of re-experiencing such pain can hinder self-confidence. Understanding that failures are stepping stones to growth and viewing them as opportunities for learning helps to overcome this barrier.

3. Comparisons and Social Expectations: Continuous comparisons with others and striving to meet societal expectations can erode self-confidence. Recognizing that everyone has unique strengths and weaknesses and focusing on personal growth rather than external validation can liberate us from this barrier.

Strategies to Cultivate Self-Confidence

Now that we have explored the significance of self-confidence and identified common barriers, let us discuss practical strategies to cultivate and strengthen it.

1. Identify and Celebrate Your Strengths: Start by acknowledging your talents and strengths. Reflect on past accomplishments and take pride in your abilities. This exercise helps shift focus from weaknesses to areas of competence, boosting self-confidence.

2. Set Realistic Goals: Setting achievable goals promotes a sense of accomplishment and reinforces self-confidence. Break down larger goals into smaller, manageable steps, allowing you to track progress and build confidence incrementally.

3. Embrace Failure and Learn from Mistakes: Failure is an inevitable part of life, but it should never define us. Embrace failures as opportunities for growth and learning, reframing them as stepping stones toward success. Analyze what went wrong, extract valuable lessons, and adjust your approach accordingly.

4. Practice Self-Compassion: Treat yourself with kindness, understanding, and forgiveness. Avoid harsh self-judgment and accept that making mistakes is part of being human. Cultivating self-compassion allows you to bounce back from setbacks and maintain

self-confidence in challenging times.

5. Surround Yourself with Positive Influences: Seek out supportive and uplifting individuals who believe in your abilities. Surrounding yourself with positivity can fortify your self-confidence and inspire you to reach for greater heights. Additionally, limit exposure to negative people or situations that drain your confidence.

6. Step Out of Your Comfort Zone: Growth occurs outside our comfort zones, and self-confidence expands with each step toward the unknown. Challenge yourself regularly by taking calculated risks and facing fears. Every successful accomplishment outside your comfort zone reinforces self-confidence.

7. Practice and Prepare: Preparation breeds confidence. Whether it is delivering a presentation, participating in a job interview, or engaging in a challenging conversation, adequate preparation instills confidence. Rehearse, research, and equip yourself with knowledge and skills to tackle situations head-on.

8. Embody Positive Body Language: Our posture and body language communicate volumes about our confidence levels. Stand tall, make eye contact, and speak clearly to exude confidence. Small changes in body language can have an immense impact on how others perceive and respond to you.

9. Maintain a Growth Mindset: Adopt a growth mindset, believing that abilities and intelligence can be developed through effort and perseverance. Embrace challenges, embrace feedback, and embrace continuous learning. A growth mindset fosters resilience, optimism, and unwavering self-confidence.

10. Celebrate Every Success: Acknowledge and reward yourself for every accomplishment, no matter how small. Celebrating success cultivates a positive mindset and reinforces your belief in your abilities. Each triumph fuels self-confidence and motivates you to tackle future endeavors.

Cultivating self-confidence is a lifelong journey that requires consistent self-awareness, self-acceptance, and intentional practice. By understanding the significance of self-confidence, identifying the barriers that inhibit its growth, and implementing the practical strategies outlined in this chapter, you can embark on a transformative path toward unwavering self-belief. Remember, self-confidence is not a destination but rather a state of mind that empowers you to conquer fears, seize opportunities, and lead a fulfilling life.

Overcoming Fear of Rejection

In this chapter, we delve into the complex realm of the fear of rejection. We will explore how it manifests, why it can have such a profound impact on our lives, and most importantly, how we can overcome it. Fear of rejection is deeply rooted in our need for acceptance and validation from others. It can constrain our personal growth, hinder our relationships, and limit our opportunities. However, with the right mindset and a willingness to confront our fears, we can break free from its shackles and embrace a more fulfilling and authentic life.

Understanding the Fear of Rejection

The fear of rejection stems from our innate desire to belong and be accepted by others. From an evolutionary standpoint, we are social beings, and our survival once hinged on being part of a group. While the modern world has evolved significantly, this deep-seated need for connection remains within us. Therefore, the prospect of being rejected can trigger a flurry of negative emotions such as anxiety, shame, and self-doubt.

However, it's important to recognize that fear of rejection is often irrational and blown out of proportion. We tend to catastrophize, assuming that rejection will lead to complete exclusion or abandonment. This exaggeration of potential consequences magnifies our anxiety, making it difficult to take risks or pursue goals.

Identifying the Sources of Fear

Acknowledging and understanding the sources of our fear of rejection is a crucial step in overcoming it. Sometimes, past experiences can shape our perception of rejection. For instance, if we have faced rejection in the past, it may leave us feeling vulnerable and wary of future encounters. This can become a self-fulfilling prophecy, where we expect rejection and unwittingly act in ways that bring about the very outcome we fear.

Additionally, societal standards and expectations play a significant role in fostering our fear of rejection. We often internalize societal messages that equate acceptance with success and worthiness. This can create a constant pressure to conform, leading us to fear being rejected when we deviate from societal norms or expectations.

Reframing Rejection as Growth

To overcome the fear of rejection, we must begin by reframing our perspective on rejection itself. Instead of viewing it as a crushing blow to our self-esteem, we can choose to see it as an opportunity for growth and learning. Each rejection serves as a valuable lesson, offering insight into what does not work or where we may need to improve.

It is essential to remind ourselves that rejection does not define us as individuals. It is merely a subjective response from someone else, influenced by their own perspective and circumstances. By shifting our focus from external validation to internal growth, we can detach our self-worth from the opinions and judgments of others.

Building Resilience and Self-Confidence

Developing resilience is key to overcoming the fear of rejection. Resilience allows us to bounce back from setbacks and rejection, rather than allowing them to define us. Building resilience requires cultivating a healthy sense of self-confidence and self-worth.

One effective strategy is to practice self-compassion. Being kind and understanding toward ourselves when faced with rejection fosters resilience and helps us maintain our self-esteem. Remind yourself that rejection is a normal part of life, and everyone experiences it at some point. Treat yourself with the same compassion and understanding you would offer a friend in a similar situation.

In addition, nurturing self-confidence involves stepping outside of our comfort zones. By gradually exposing ourselves to situations that may result in rejection, we become more resilient and less fearful.

Start small, perhaps by initiating conversations with new people or taking on new challenges. With each small success, our confidence grows, empowering us to face larger rejections with a more positive mindset.

Challenging Negative Beliefs

Our fear of rejection often stems from negative beliefs we hold about ourselves. These beliefs become self-fulfilling prophecies, as we inadvertently project our insecurities onto others and interpret their actions through a negative lens. Overcoming this cycle requires actively challenging and reframing these negative beliefs.

Begin by identifying the negative thoughts that arise when faced with the possibility of rejection. For example, "I am unworthy," or "I will never be accepted." Then, consciously question the evidence supporting these beliefs. Are these thoughts based on facts, or are they distorted interpretations?

Replace these negative beliefs with more balanced and realistic affirmations. Affirmations such as "I am deserving of love and acceptance," or "I have unique qualities to offer" can help rewire our mindset and build self-confidence.

Developing Authenticity and Vulnerability

A key aspect of overcoming the fear of rejection is embracing authenticity and vulnerability. Many times, we put up defensive walls and wear masks to protect ourselves from potential rejection.

However, this self-protection limits our ability to form genuine connections and inhibits our personal growth.

Authenticity is about being true to ourselves, expressing our genuine thoughts, feelings, and desires. When we embrace authenticity, we attract people who appreciate and accept us for who we truly are. This builds stronger and more meaningful relationships, reducing the fear of rejection.

Vulnerability involves allowing ourselves to be seen, flaws and all. It is through vulnerability that we establish deeper connections with others. By sharing our fears, insecurities, and past rejections with trusted individuals, we realize that rejection does not have to be isolating. Instead, it can foster empathy, understanding, and stronger bonds.

Overcoming the fear of rejection is a process that requires self-reflection, self-compassion, and a willingness to challenge negative beliefs. By reframing rejection as an opportunity for growth, building resilience and self-confidence, challenging negative beliefs, and embracing authenticity and vulnerability, we can overcome this fear and experience deeper connections and personal fulfillment.

Remember, everyone faces rejection at some point in their lives. It is a natural part of the human experience. The difference lies in how we perceive and respond to rejection. By developing the tools and mindset discussed in this chapter, you can navigate the fear of rejection and emerge stronger, more confident, and capable of creating the life you desire.

Setting Boundaries

In our journey through life, we often find ourselves faced with situations and people that can drain our energy and leave us feeling overwhelmed. Whether it's a demanding job, an overbearing friend, or a toxic family member, it becomes essential to establish clear boundaries to protect our mental and emotional well-being. In this chapter, we will explore the importance of setting boundaries, different types of boundaries, and practical strategies to implement them effectively in our lives.

Understanding Boundaries:

Boundaries can be defined as the invisible lines that we draw around ourselves to define what is acceptable and what is not in our interactions with others. They serve as guidelines for how we allow ourselves to be treated and how we treat others. Setting boundaries is not about controlling or manipulating others; rather, it is about taking responsibility for our own needs and prioritizing self-care.

Types of Boundaries:

Boundaries can be categorized into four main types: physical, emotional, intellectual, and spiritual. Each type serves a distinct purpose and contributes to our overall well-being.

1. Physical Boundaries: These boundaries determine how close or far people can come into our personal space. They include physical touch, personal belongings, and privacy. For example, some individuals may have strict physical boundaries and feel uncomfortable with hugs or handshakes, while others may have more relaxed boundaries.

2. Emotional Boundaries: Emotional boundaries involve establishing limits on how much emotional information we share with others and how much we allow others to share with us. It's about maintaining a healthy level of emotional autonomy and privacy. Setting emotional boundaries helps prevent emotional manipulation and promotes emotional well-being.

3. Intellectual Boundaries: Intellectual boundaries protect our thoughts, opinions, and ideas. They involve being open to different perspectives while also respecting our own intellectual beliefs. By setting intellectual boundaries, we can engage in healthy debates and discussions without feeling attacked or invalidated.

4. Spiritual Boundaries: Spiritual boundaries pertain to our values, beliefs, and faith. They help us maintain a sense of integrity and protect us from being coerced into compromising our spiritual principles. By setting spiritual boundaries, we can explore and grow spiritually in a way that aligns with our authentic selves.

Why Set Boundaries?

Setting boundaries is crucial for our mental, emotional, and physical well-being. Here are some key reasons why setting boundaries is essential in our lives:

1. Self-Care: By setting boundaries, we prioritize our own needs, allowing us to maintain a healthy balance between giving and receiving. Boundaries ensure that we have enough time and energy for self-care activities that nurture and replenish us.

2. Healthy Relationships: Boundaries play a vital role in fostering healthy relationships. They provide clarity and mutual understanding, making it easier to navigate conflicts and respect each other's needs. Clear boundaries promote open communication, trust, and respect within relationships.

3. Personal Growth: Setting boundaries requires self-reflection and self-awareness. It encourages us to evaluate our needs, values, and limits. Through this process, we gain a better understanding of ourselves and grow as individuals.

4. Emotional Well-being: Boundaries protect us from emotional manipulation, intrusion, and draining relationships. They help us maintain emotional autonomy, preventing us from becoming overly dependent on others for validation or happiness.

Strategies for Setting Boundaries:

Now that we understand the significance of boundaries, let's explore some practical strategies for setting and implementing them effectively:

1. Self-Reflection: Begin by assessing your needs, values, and limits. Reflect on situations or relationships where you feel overwhelmed or taken advantage of. Understanding your boundaries will lay the foundation for setting them.

2. Communicate Clearly: Clearly express your boundaries to others, using "I" statements to avoid sounding accusatory or aggressive. For example, instead of saying, "You always invade my privacy," say, "I need some personal space and would appreciate it if you could respect that."

3. Learn to Say No: Saying "no" is an important part of setting boundaries. Practice asserting yourself and declining requests or activities that go against your boundaries. Remember, it's okay to prioritize your well-being.

4. Practice Self-Care: Prioritize self-care activities that nourish your mind, body, and soul. Set aside time for hobbies, relaxation, exercise, and engaging in activities that bring you joy. Self-care is not selfish; it is a necessary investment in your overall well-being.

5. Seek Support: Surround yourself with individuals who respect and understand your boundaries. Seek support from friends, family, or professionals, such as therapists or coaches, who can provide guidance and encouragement.

Setting boundaries is a powerful and necessary step towards cultivating a fulfilling and balanced life. It allows us to take control of our well-being, nurture healthy relationships, and grow as individuals. By establishing and maintaining clear boundaries, we create an environment in which we can thrive, cultivate self-worth, and embrace the authentic versions of ourselves. Remember, setting boundaries is an ongoing process that requires self-awareness, practice, and self-compassion. Embrace this journey as you learn to protect and prioritize your mental, emotional, and physical well-being.

Constructive Conflict Resolution

Conflict is an inevitable part of our lives. Whether it is in our personal relationships, professional settings, or societal dynamics, conflicts arise when interests, ideas, or values collide. Many view conflict as inherently negative, as it often leads to tension, stress, and strained relationships. However, conflicts can also be opportunities for growth, learning, and transformation, provided we approach them with a constructive mindset and apply effective conflict resolution strategies. In this chapter, we will delve into the world of constructive conflict resolution, exploring the principles, techniques, and skills necessary to navigate conflicts successfully.

Understanding Conflict

Before we embark on our journey towards constructive conflict resolution, it is essential to understand the nature and dynamics of conflicts. Broadly defined, conflict refers to a struggle resulting from incompatible desires, needs, or actions. However, conflicts can take various forms and manifest at different levels, such as intrapersonal, interpersonal, intergroup, or international.

Intrapersonal conflicts occur within an individual's mind, often involving conflicting thoughts, emotions, or values. Learning how to manage and resolve these internal conflicts is a crucial step towards addressing external conflicts effectively. On the other hand, interpersonal conflicts occur between individuals, arising from differences in attitudes, beliefs, or goals. These conflicts may be personal, professional, or even related to societal issues.

Additionally, conflicts can emerge at a broader level, such as intergroup conflicts between different teams or departments in an organization or international conflicts between nations. While the dynamics and complexities vary across different levels, the principles of constructive conflict resolution remain applicable in each context.

The Benefits of Constructive Conflict Resolution

Conflict resolution is a skill that many individuals and societies struggle with, often resorting to destructive ways of handling conflicts. However, embracing constructive conflict resolution practices holds numerous benefits for individuals and communities alike.

Firstly, when conflicts are managed constructively, they serve as catalysts for personal and interpersonal growth. By engaging in dialogue, listening to others' perspectives, and expressing their own opinions respectfully, individuals can develop a deeper understanding of themselves and others. Through conflict resolution, individuals can learn to recognize and manage their emotions, fostering self-awareness and emotional intelligence.

Furthermore, constructive conflict resolution builds stronger relationships. When conflicts are resolved positively, it promotes trust, respect, and empathy among individuals. By resolving conflicts openly and transparently, it paves the way for improved communication and collaboration, leading to better relationships in personal and professional spheres.

Constructive conflict resolution is also instrumental in fostering innovation. Conflicts often arise when different viewpoints clash, but by encouraging diverse perspectives and allowing open dialogue, conflicts can spark creativity and innovative solutions. Approaching conflicts as opportunities for new insights and growth enables individuals and organizations to explore alternative ideas and methods, leading to positive change and progress.

Principles of Constructive Conflict Resolution

In order to approach conflicts constructively, it is essential to embrace some fundamental principles that guide the process of conflict resolution. These principles lay the groundwork for effective communication, understanding, and collaboration.

1. Remain Calm: Conflict situations can often be emotionally charged, making it crucial to maintain a sense of calmness. Emotional

reactions can cloud judgment and hinder effective communication. By managing our emotions and approaching conflicts with a calm mindset, we can create an atmosphere conducive to constructive resolution.

2. Active Listening: Listening is one of the key skills required for successful conflict resolution. It involves giving our full attention to the other person, seeking to understand their perspective without interruption or judgment. By actively listening, we can uncover underlying concerns, needs, and values, fostering empathy and mutual understanding.

3. Respect Differences: Recognizing and respecting the diversity of opinions, beliefs, and values is essential in conflict resolution. Rather than trying to impose our own viewpoint, we should acknowledge the validity of others' perspectives. Embracing the concept that differences can coexist without erasing our own values allows us to find common ground and build bridges.

4. Focus on Interests, not Positions: Often, conflicts arise from an attachment to fixed positions or solutions. In order to move towards resolution, it is important to shift the focus towards understanding each party's underlying interests and needs. By exploring the motivations and desires behind the positions, we can identify mutually beneficial solutions that satisfy both parties.

5. Collaborative Problem-Solving: Constructive conflict resolution aims for win-win solutions. By adopting a collaborative mindset, parties can work together to find creative solutions that address all parties' interests. This approach encourages brainstorming, exploring alternatives, and finding compromises that go beyond a zero-sum mindset.

Techniques for Constructive Conflict Resolution

Implementing the principles of constructive conflict resolution often requires specific techniques to navigate conflicts effectively. While different conflicts demand tailored approaches, the following techniques can serve as valuable tools in resolving conflicts constructively.

1. Communication and Dialogue: Open and honest communication is at the core of constructive conflict resolution. Through dialogue, parties can express their concerns, feelings, and needs, while actively listening to others. It is important to create an environment where all parties feel safe to share their perspectives without fear of judgment or reprisal.

2. Empathy and Understanding: Empathy involves putting ourselves in the other person's shoes, striving to understand their experiences and emotions. By demonstrating empathy towards others, we foster a sense of connection and understanding. This paves the way for

collaborative problem-solving, as it encourages mutual empathy and recognition of shared humanity.

3. Mediation and Facilitation: In situations where conflicts seem insurmountable, involving a neutral third party can be beneficial. A mediator or facilitator can help guide the process of conflict resolution, ensuring fair and effective communication, and promoting collaborative solutions. Their role involves fostering dialogue, highlighting common interests, and reframing conflicts in a positive light.

4. Negotiation and Compromise: Negotiation involves finding common ground by bargaining and seeking mutually agreeable solutions. It requires a give-and-take approach, where parties are willing to compromise in order to reach a resolution. Negotiation skills, such as setting clear objectives, exploring alternatives, and effective communication, play a crucial role in constructive conflict resolution.

5. Conflict Transformation: In cases where conflicts seem deeply entrenched, conflict transformation offers an alternative approach. Rather than seeking a win-lose outcome, conflict transformation aims to fundamentally change the dynamics and underlying causes of the conflict. It involves addressing root causes, building relationships, and fostering long-term change through collaboration and peacebuilding efforts.

Conflict is an integral part of human existence, but it is our approach to conflict resolution that determines whether conflicts become destructive or constructive forces. By embracing constructive conflict resolution principles, techniques, and skills, individuals and communities can navigate conflicts with empathy, understanding, and collaboration. Constructive conflict resolution fosters personal growth, strengthens relationships, and paves the way for innovative solutions. It is a journey that requires patience, open-mindedness, and a willingness to engage in dialogue, but the rewards are immense. As we embark on this journey towards constructive conflict resolution, let us remember that conflicts can be turned into opportunities for transformation, growth, and positive change.

Chapter 4: Effective Communication Strategies

In today's fast-paced and interconnected world, effective communication has become more crucial than ever before. Whether in personal relationships, professional settings, or even simple day-to-day interactions, the ability to express thoughts and ideas clearly and concisely can make all the difference.

In this chapter, we will delve into the various strategies and techniques that can enhance our communication skills. We will explore the importance of active listening, non-verbal cues, empathetic communication, and effective questioning. These concepts are applicable across different contexts and can greatly improve our ability to convey messages accurately and build strong connections with others.

Active Listening: The Foundation of Effective Communication

Listening is a skill that often goes overlooked in the communication process. Many individuals mistakenly believe that communication is primarily about speaking and expressing oneself. However, active listening plays a pivotal role in understanding others, fostering empathy, and facilitating meaningful conversations.

Active listening involves focusing on the speaker, fully comprehending their message, and responding appropriately. To become an active listener, one must avoid distractions, both external and internal, and provide undivided attention to the speaker. This includes maintaining eye contact, nodding or using other non-verbal cues to indicate understanding, and refraining from interrupting.

Paraphrasing, or restating the speaker's message in your own words, is another valuable technique in active listening. This helps confirm understanding and allows the speaker to clarify any misinterpretations. By practicing active listening, we create an atmosphere of respect and open-mindedness, enabling effective communication to take place.

Non-Verbal Cues: The Silent Messengers

Communication is not limited to words alone. Non-verbal cues such as body language, facial expressions, and tone of voice convey a wealth of information about our thoughts and emotions. Understanding and effectively utilizing these non-verbal cues can significantly enhance the impact of our message.

Body language, for instance, includes gestures, postures, and movements that can either reinforce or contradict the spoken words. A relaxed and open posture can create a sense of approachability, while crossed arms may convey defensiveness or resistance. Similarly, maintaining eye contact and nodding in agreement can signal active engagement and attentiveness.

Facial expressions are another powerful form of non-verbal communication. A genuine smile can project warmth and sincerity, while a furrowed brow may indicate confusion or concern. By consciously monitoring our own non-verbal cues and being attuned to those of others, we can align our messages holistically and avoid any inconsistencies.

Tone of voice is yet another non-verbal aspect that can profoundly impact communication. The way we speak, the pitch, and the cadence all add layers of meaning to our words. The same sentence can convey different messages depending on the tone used. By mastering the art of tone, we can effectively express empathy, assertiveness, or urgency, as appropriate for the situation.

Empathetic Communication: Bridging the Gap

Effective communication requires more than just transmitting messages accurately; it necessitates empathetic understanding. Empathy is the ability to genuinely comprehend and share another person's feelings, connecting on a deeper level. Empathetic communication is the key to building trust, resolving conflicts, and fostering strong relationships.

To establish empathy in communication, it is crucial to actively listen and remain non-judgmental. Put yourself in the speaker's shoes, attempt to understand their perspective, and acknowledge their emotions. Validating someone's feelings contributes to a safe and supportive environment, encouraging open and honest dialogue.

Empathetic communication also involves being mindful of our own emotions and responses. It requires managing our biases and ego, ensuring that our personal experiences do not overshadow or invalidate the experiences of others. By embracing empathy, we can promote understanding, empathy, and inclusivity in our interactions.

Effective Questioning: The Art of Inquiry

Asking the right questions can uncover crucial information, deepen understanding, and stimulate meaningful conversations. Effective questioning involves constructing queries that are clear, concise, and purposeful. It encourages reflection and promotes active engagement between participants.

Open-ended questions are particularly useful in eliciting detailed responses, encouraging someone to share their thoughts and feelings. These questions typically begin with words like "what," "how," or "why," inviting the speaker to express themselves freely. Closed-ended questions, on the other hand, require a simple "yes" or "no" answer and should be used sparingly to avoid stifling discussion.

The art of effective questioning also involves active listening and adapting the line of inquiry accordingly. Asking follow-up questions, seeking clarification, or summarizing the speaker's main points are valuable techniques to demonstrate genuine interest and facilitate deeper understanding.

Effective communication strategies are essential in navigating the various interactions we encounter daily. Active listening, non-verbal cues, empathetic communication, and effective questioning are powerful tools that can enhance our ability to convey messages accurately and build meaningful connections with others.
By practicing these strategies, we can foster open and honest communication, bridge gaps in understanding, and promote empathy and inclusion. Effective communication is a lifelong skill that requires continuous learning and practice, and it is one that can positively transform our personal and professional relationships.

'I' Statements

Effective communication is an essential tool for building and maintaining healthy relationships. It has the power to resolve conflicts, express emotions, and foster understanding. However, not all communication styles are created equal. In this chapter, we will delve into 'I' statements, a powerful technique that can enhance meaningful conversations. By using 'I' statements, individuals can express their thoughts, feelings, and needs in a non-confrontational and constructive manner. Throughout this chapter, we will explore the benefits, applications, and examples of 'I' statements, helping you harness this valuable tool to improve your communication skills.

4.1.1 The Power of 'I' Statements

Imagine the following scenario: Sarah and John have been dating for a few months and have recently moved in together. Due to their contrasting work schedules, they often find it challenging to spend quality time together. Sarah, who feels neglected and unimportant, decides to talk to John about her concerns. She has two options. She can choose to use a blameful communication style, saying, "You never make time for me. You prioritize work over our relationship!" Or, she can employ an 'I' statement, which might sound like, "I feel neglected and unimportant when we don't spend quality time together."

In this example, it is clear that the second approach is more likely to elicit a positive response from John. By using an 'I' statement, Sarah avoids placing blame on John, allowing him to better understand her feelings without feeling defensive. The power of 'I' statements lies in their ability to express personal experiences and emotions, making them an invaluable tool for effective communication.

When we use 'I' statements, we take ownership of our thoughts and feelings. It is fundamental to remember that nobody can dispute our personal experiences because they are uniquely ours. By avoiding accusatory or judgmental language, we can create a more open and safe conversation space where both parties can express their viewpoints honestly and without fear of reprisal.

4.1.2 Applying 'I' Statements

Now that we understand the underlying principles and advantages of 'I' statements, let us examine how we can effectively apply them in everyday situations. Whether it is personal relationships, professional settings, or even interactions with strangers, incorporating 'I' statements can help us express ourselves assertively and enhance the quality of our conversations.

In personal relationships, such as marriages, friendships, or family dynamics, 'I' statements play a crucial role in addressing conflicts and fostering harmony. For instance, imagine a disagreement between two siblings, Alex and Emily, regarding the division of household chores. Instead of blaming each other and escalating the argument, they could each use 'I' statements to express their concerns. Alex might say, "I feel overwhelmed and burdened when I am solely responsible for all the household chores." Emily, in response, could say, "I feel frustrated and unappreciated when I perceive a lack of effort from others in sharing the household responsibilities." By using 'I' statements, both individuals open up a dialogue focused on their feelings and experiences, ultimately paving the way for a more constructive and empathetic conversation.

In professional settings, the use of 'I' statements can help navigate conflicts, difficult conversations, and negotiations. For instance, within a team, a project deadline might be at risk due to misunderstandings and miscommunication. Instead of pointing fingers, team members can employ 'I' statements to express their concerns and suggest improvements. One team member might say, "I feel anxious and concerned about the approaching deadline. I believe we could benefit from clearer communication and more defined roles." This approach allows team members to focus on solutions rather than blame, fostering a more collaborative and productive environment.

On a broader scale, 'I' statements can also be utilized in societal conversations and debates. When discussing sensitive issues, such as politics, race, or gender, expressing ourselves with 'I' statements can help create empathy and avoid defensive responses. For instance, instead of making statements that generalize or label individuals, we can say, "I feel frustrated and disappointed when I witness incidents of racism or discrimination." By emphasizing our individual experiences rather than attacking others' beliefs, we open the door to thought-provoking discussions that promote understanding and growth.

4.1.3 Examples of 'I' Statements

To further understand how 'I' statements are utilized, let us explore a variety of examples applicable to various scenarios. These examples will assist you in adopting this communication technique effectively.

1. Relationship Example:
"I feel hurt and unvalued when our plans keep getting canceled without prior notice. I would appreciate more consideration for my time and feelings."

2. Parent-Child Example:
"I feel worried and concerned when you come home late without informing me. It would help if we could establish better communication to ensure your safety and my peace of mind."

3. Work Example:

"I feel overwhelmed and unsupported when I am assigned multiple tasks without clear priorities or adequate resources. I believe establishing better coordination and delegation would lead to improved efficiency."

4. Conflict Resolution Example:

"I feel frustrated and disrespected when you interrupt me while I am speaking. I hope we can find a way to communicate without talking over each other to ensure that both of our viewpoints are heard and respected."

5. Team Collaboration Example:

"I feel confused and left out when decisions are made without my input. I believe that involving everyone in the decision-making process can foster a more inclusive and effective team dynamic."

In each of these examples, the use of 'I' statements allows individuals to express their emotions, concerns, and needs assertively without placing blame or accusation on others. This technique avoids escalating conflicts and facilitates a more conducive atmosphere for meaningful discussions and problem-solving.

4.1.4 Challenges and Limitations

While 'I' statements offer a powerful tool for effective

communication, it is important to recognize that they may not be a solution for every situation. Like any communication technique, 'I' statements have their limitations and may face challenges in certain contexts.

One challenge is that individuals may not be accustomed to expressing themselves using 'I' statements. People often rely on accusatory or generalizing language as a learned behavior passed down through generations or acquired through various social influences. Overcoming this challenge requires practice, patience, and an understanding of the benefits associated with 'I' statements. By consciously incorporating this technique into our communication, we can gradually develop a more constructive and empathetic approach.

Another limitation arises when individuals use 'I' statements as a means of passive-aggression or manipulation. Even though 'I' statements are intended to express personal experiences, they can be twisted for ulterior motives. It is crucial to remain authentic and genuine while using 'I' statements, focusing on expressing emotions and needs rather than using them as a means of manipulation or control.

Additionally, some cultures and societal norms may view the use of 'I' statements as confrontational or self-centered. It is essential to recognize and adapt communication strategies to honor cultural differences and respect the context in which we are communicating. Adapting our approach without compromising our authenticity and emotional expression allows us to foster understanding and connection across diverse backgrounds.

Despite these challenges and limitations, 'I' statements remain a powerful and valuable tool for effective communication. By practicing and incorporating them into our daily interactions, we can improve our relationships, resolve conflicts, and create a more harmonious and empathetic world.

In this section has explored the concept and application of 'I' statements as an essential communication technique. We discussed their power to express personal thoughts, feelings, and needs in a non-confrontational manner, enhancing understanding and fostering empathy. Through various examples, we witnessed the practicality of 'I' statements in personal relationships, workplaces, and broader societal conversations. However, we must acknowledge the challenges and limitations associated with their implementation. By embracing 'I' statements, practicing authentic expression, and adapting our approach to respect cultural differences, we can elevate our communication skills and build stronger connections with others. Remember, effective communication starts with the self, and 'I' statements empower us to articulate our truth while maintaining open-hearted dialogue.

Active Listening

In today's fast-paced and interconnected world, effective communication has become more important than ever. Whether at work, in relationships, or even during casual conversations, the ability to truly listen and understand others is a vital skill. Yet, despite its significance, many of us struggle with active listening, often falling into the trap of waiting for our turn to speak rather than genuinely engaging with the speaker. This chapter will delve into the art of active listening, exploring its importance, benefits, and practical techniques that can be employed to enhance this essential skill.

Understanding Active Listening

Active listening is more than mere hearing; it involves fully engaging with the speaker and processing their words, tone, and body language. It is about providing undivided attention and showing genuine interest in what is being communicated. Active listening promotes effective communication by fostering trust, understanding, and empathy between individuals.

Benefits of Active Listening

Before delving into the techniques of active listening, it is crucial to understand the myriad benefits it brings. At its core, active listening serves to enhance relationships. By actively engaging with others, we demonstrate our respect and value for their thoughts and feelings, leading to stronger interpersonal connections. Furthermore, active listening allows us to gain a deeper understanding of the speaker's needs, concerns, and perspectives, enabling us to respond more effectively and appropriately.

Active listening also contributes to personal growth. By attentively listening to others, we expose ourselves to different ideas and experiences, broadening our horizons and enhancing our knowledge. The insights gained through active listening can be invaluable in personal and professional development, providing us with new perspectives and fostering creativity.

Techniques for Active Listening

1. Give your undivided attention: Active listening begins by eliminating distractions and giving the speaker your full attention. Put away your phone, turn off the TV, and make eye contact with the speaker. By displaying genuine interest, you create an environment of trust and respect, encouraging the speaker to open up.

2. Practice empathy: Empathy is crucial in active listening. Strive to put yourself in the speaker's shoes, attempting to understand their perspective and emotions. This empathetic mindset allows you to

connect on a deeper level, fostering mutual understanding.

3. Provide verbal and non-verbal cues: Active listening involves conveying your engagement through both verbal and non-verbal cues. Nodding, maintaining appropriate eye contact, and using encouraging gestures such as leaning forward, all demonstrate your attentiveness and encourage the speaker to continue sharing their thoughts.

4. Avoid interrupting: Interrupting the speaker is a common pitfall in communication. Instead of waiting for your turn to speak or formulating responses, focus on absorbing what the speaker is saying. By giving them their due space, you show respect and foster an environment where they feel heard.

5. Reflect and paraphrase: To confirm your understanding and show the speaker that you are actively listening, periodically reflect and paraphrase their main points. Restating their ideas in your own words not only demonstrates that you are fully engaged but also ensures that you correctly interpret their message.

6. Respond appropriately: Active listening is incomplete without appropriate responses. Once the speaker has finished expressing themselves, respond with empathy and respect. Avoid judging or dismissing their opinions, even if you disagree. Instead, offer constructive feedback and engage in meaningful dialogue that

furthers the conversation.

7. Ask clarifying questions: If you find yourself unclear about something the speaker has said, do not hesitate to ask clarifying questions. It shows your willingness to understand their message thoroughly and demonstrates your commitment to active listening.

8. Be mindful of your body language: Your body language plays a significant role in active listening. Maintain an open posture, facing the speaker, and avoid crossing your arms or legs, as this may signal defensiveness or disinterest. By consciously adjusting your body language, you create an atmosphere conducive to honest and open conversation.

Challenges and Overcoming Barriers

While active listening offers many benefits, it also presents its fair share of challenges. It is crucial to be aware of these obstacles and employ strategies to overcome them.

One common challenge is the tendency to become distracted by internal thoughts or personal biases. To combat this, practice mindful listening, grounding yourself in the present moment and actively refocusing on the speaker's words whenever your mind starts to wander.

Another obstacle is the impulse to offer immediate solutions or advice. Often, we are so eager to help that we forget the primary purpose of active listening – to provide a safe space for the speaker to express themselves fully. By resisting this urge and focusing on understanding the speaker's perspective first, we can better support them when the time for guidance arises.

Lastly, cultural and language barriers can hinder active listening. Differences in communication styles and language proficiency may result in misinterpretation or misunderstanding. In such scenarios, patience, openness, and a willingness to seek clarification become essential tools to overcome these challenges and facilitate effective communication.

Active listening is an art that requires patience, practice, and a genuine desire to connect with others. By employing the techniques and strategies outlined in this chapter, you can transform your listening skills, fostering deeper relationships, gaining new insights, and enhancing personal growth. Remember, true understanding is nurtured through active engagement, and by becoming a skilled active listener, you will not only improve your own communication but also inspire others to do the same.

Asking Clarifying Questions

In our day-to-day lives, effective communication plays a crucial role in building strong relationships and achieving success in various aspects. One essential element that often goes overlooked in communication is the art of asking clarifying questions. The ability to ask thoughtful questions allows us to gain a deeper understanding, resolve conflicts, and find creative solutions. In this chapter, we will explore the power of asking clarifying questions and provide practical strategies to enhance your communication skills.

Section 1: The Importance of Clarifying Questions

1.1 Enhancing Understanding:

Have you ever found yourself in a situation where you misunderstood someone's message? Misinterpretations can lead to confusion, frustration, and even conflict. By asking clarifying questions, we can avoid these pitfalls and ensure that we comprehend the intended message accurately. Clarification questions help us fill in missing information, gain more context, and actively engage in meaningful conversations.

1.2 Resolving Conflicts:

Conflict is an inevitable part of life, whether at work, within relationships, or in social settings. Misunderstandings and unaddressed assumptions often contribute to conflicts. By asking clarifying questions, we can uncover hidden motives, address differing perspectives, and resolve conflicts more effectively. Through this process, we demonstrate empathy towards others' viewpoints and create a safe environment for open dialogue.

1.3 Encouraging Active Listening:

Asking clarifying questions helps foster active listening, a crucial skill in effective communication. When we ask questions, we show genuine interest in the speaker's perspective, encouraging them to open up and share more. This not only enhances our understanding but also makes the speaker feel valued and heard. Active listening builds trust and strengthens relationships, paving the way for meaningful connections.

Section 2: Types of Clarifying Questions

2.1 Open-Ended Questions:

Open-ended questions are designed to encourage an in-depth response from the speaker. They cannot be answered with a simple "yes" or "no" and require the speaker to provide more elaborate information. Open-ended questions often start with words like "What," "How," or "Tell me about." These questions allow individuals to express themselves freely and provide essential details that may not emerge with closed-ended questions.

For example, instead of asking, "Did you like the event?" you can ask, "What were your thoughts and feelings about the event?"

2.2 Closed-Ended Questions:

Closed-ended questions, on the other hand, require concise answers and can often be answered with a simple "yes" or "no." They are useful when seeking specific information or confirming facts. While closed-ended questions may not encourage a deep conversation, they serve a purpose in obtaining quick and specific answers.

For example, if you need to confirm someone's availability for a meeting, you could ask, "Can you attend the meeting at 3 pm tomorrow?"

2.3 Probing Questions:

Probing questions are designed to delve deeper into a specific topic or issue. These questions help to uncover underlying thoughts, motivations, or more detailed information. Probing questions often begin with phrases such as "Why," "Could you explain further," or "What led you to that conclusion?" By using probing questions, we demonstrate our genuine curiosity and encourage others to share more in-depth insights.

For instance, if someone mentions they are unhappy at work, a probing question could be, "What specifically about your work environment is contributing to your unhappiness?"

Section 3: Effective Strategies for Asking Clarifying Questions

3.1 Active Listening:

Active listening is the foundation of effective communication and asking clarifying questions. To ask meaningful questions, we must first listen attentively to the speaker. Active listening involves avoiding distractions, maintaining eye contact, and being fully present in the conversation. When we truly listen, we can identify areas that require clarification and ask appropriate questions to gain a better understanding.

3.2 Summarizing and Paraphrasing:

Summarizing or paraphrasing what the speaker has said is an effective strategy to demonstrate comprehension and elicit further clarification. By rephrasing the speaker's message in our own words, we confirm our understanding and give them an opportunity to either affirm or correct our interpretation. Summarizing also helps to consolidate information and identify any gaps that need clarification.

3.3 Non-Judgmental Approach:

Asking clarifying questions requires us to adopt a non-judgmental attitude. It is important to approach conversations with an open mind, free from preconceived notions or biases. By refraining from passing judgment or making assumptions, we create a safe space for honest and open communication. This approach encourages individuals to share their thoughts candidly, without fear of being misunderstood or judged.

3.4 Using Empathy:

Empathy is a powerful tool when asking clarifying questions. It allows us to understand the speaker's perspective, emotions, and experiences on a deeper level. When we empathize, we are better able to ask thoughtful questions that uncover underlying reasons, challenges, or concerns. By showing empathy, we build rapport and enhance the quality of our interactions.

Asking clarifying questions is an essential skill that can transform the way we communicate and connect with others. By embracing active listening, demonstrating empathy, and using various question types, we can enhance our understanding, resolve conflicts, and foster meaningful relationships. Practice incorporating clarifying questions into your conversations, and you will discover the countless benefits it brings to your personal and professional life.

Using Positive Language

In the realm of communication, the manner in which we express ourselves plays a vital role in influencing how others perceive us. Using positive language forms the cornerstone of effective communication and can significantly impact our personal and professional relationships. This chapter explores the power of positive language, its benefits, and how we can cultivate this skill to enhance our interactions with others.

The Power of Words

Words possess an incredible power that can either uplift or diminish those around us. Research has shown that positive language can enhance relationships, boost morale, and promote productivity. Conversely, negative language can have detrimental effects on individuals, fostering an environment of hostility and demotivation.

Choosing to focus on positive language is not only beneficial for the recipients of our messages, but it also profoundly impacts us as speakers. By consciously using positive words and expressions, we improve our own well-being, increase our self-confidence, and foster a more optimistic outlook on life.

Understanding Positivity

Before we delve into the strategies of using positive language, it is crucial to understand what positivity truly entails. Positivity encompasses more than just the absence of negative words or criticism; it is an approach to communication that embraces empathy, encouragement, and constructive feedback.

By adopting a positive mindset, we cultivate an atmosphere of support, collaboration, and growth. Our words become tools for building bridges rather than barriers, fostering understanding instead of conflict.

Benefits of Positive Language

Using positive language is not a mere superficial act; it yields numerous tangible benefits in both personal and professional settings. Let us explore some of the advantages of integrating positive language into our everyday interactions:

1. Improved relationships: Positive language strengthens our connections with others, deepening understanding and trust. Instead of focusing solely on problems, we emphasize solutions and possibilities, fostering an environment of collaboration and support.

2. Enhanced productivity: Consistently using positive language at

work encourages an atmosphere of motivation and engagement. Employees are more likely to feel valued and inspired, leading to increased productivity and a sense of accomplishment.

3. Conflict resolution: Positive language aids in conflict resolution as it allows us to address sensitive topics with empathy and understanding. By using words that promote open dialogue and mutual respect, we are more likely to find constructive solutions.

4. Boosted self-confidence: Both as speakers and listeners, positive language enhances our self-confidence. By employing words of encouragement and affirmation, we foster a belief in our abilities, leading to increased resilience and improved performance.

Strategies for Using Positive Language

Now that we understand the power and benefits of positive language, let us explore practical strategies for incorporating it into our daily communication:

1. Mindful self-awareness: The first step in using positive language is self-awareness. We must recognize our own patterns of communication, identify areas for improvement, and make a conscious effort to adjust our language accordingly. Awareness allows us to better understand how our words impact others and, most importantly, ourselves.

2. Replace negative words with positive alternatives: Instead of focusing on what is wrong, shift your perspective to highlight what is right. Replace negative words such as "can't" with positive alternatives like "can" or "will." This simple change in vocabulary can have a profound impact on our mindset and the atmosphere of our conversations.

3. Empathy and active listening: Demonstrating empathy and active listening skills allows us to create an understanding and supportive environment. By genuinely connecting with others and validating their feelings and experiences, we enhance our ability to respond with positive language.

4. Use words that inspire and motivate: Positive language is not limited to mere pleasantries; it also involves using words that inspire, motivate, and empower. By actively seeking opportunities to provide encouragement and celebrate achievements, we uplift others and create a culture of positivity.

5. Be solution-oriented: When faced with challenges, focusing on solutions instead of dwelling on problems is crucial. Positive language emphasizes possibilities and encourages brainstorming for effective resolutions. By shifting our mindset towards finding proactive solutions, we inspire others to approach challenges creatively.

6. Practice mindfulness and gratitude: Incorporating mindfulness and gratitude into our communication helps us foster positivity. Taking a moment to appreciate and acknowledge the efforts of others through words of gratitude strengthens our relationships and creates an atmosphere of appreciation.

By consciously embracing positive language in our interactions, we wield the power to transform our relationships, our workplaces, and ourselves. The strategies discussed in this chapter are only a steppingstone towards creating a more harmonious and supportive communication style.

Remember, cultivating positive language begins with self-awareness and a genuine desire to connect with others on a more profound level. With every word we choose, we have the power to uplift, inspire, and foster growth. Let us embark on this journey towards positive communication and witness the transformative effects it has on our lives.

Chapter 5: Navigating Difficult Conversations

In every aspect of our lives, there are moments when we find ourselves facing difficult conversations. These conversations can arise in the workplace, within personal relationships, or even during casual interactions with acquaintances. Navigating these conversations can be challenging, as they often involve sensitive subjects, conflicting opinions, and intense emotions. In this chapter, we will explore various strategies and tools that will help you navigate through difficult conversations with empathy, clarity, and understanding.

Understanding Difficult Conversations:

Before delving into the techniques and strategies to navigate difficult conversations, it is essential to comprehend what makes these conversations challenging. Difficult conversations typically arise when individuals hold differing viewpoints or when emotions run high. These conversations may involve delivering or receiving criticism, discussing sensitive topics, or addressing conflicts. The key to successful navigation lies in understanding that difficult conversations are an inevitable part of life and that they can often lead to personal growth and improved relationships when handled thoughtfully.

Preparing for a Difficult Conversation:

Preparing yourself mentally and emotionally is crucial before entering any difficult conversation. Start by understanding your own emotions and motivations behind having the conversation. Ask yourself what outcome you hope to achieve, and consider your intentions and desired goals. This self-awareness will allow you to approach the conversation with empathy and clarity, ensuring a more balanced and productive dialogue.

Effective Communication Techniques:

1. Active Listening:

Active listening forms the foundation of successful communication in any conversation, particularly in difficult ones. When engaging in a difficult conversation, it is essential to give the other person your full attention. Maintain eye contact, nod to show understanding, and avoid interrupting. Demonstrate empathy by reflecting back the other person's feelings and concerns. By actively listening, you not only convey respect but also gain valuable insights into the other person's perspective, paving the way for effective resolution.

2. Empathy and Understanding:

Difficult conversations are often emotionally charged, and acknowledging the other person's feelings is crucial. Show empathy by trying to understand their experience and perspective. Put yourself in their shoes and try to grasp their emotions and concerns.

This empathetic approach fosters a safe environment and builds trust, facilitating an open and honest dialogue.

3. Use "I" Statements:

When expressing your thoughts or concerns during a difficult conversation, using "I" statements can prevent the conversation from becoming accusatory or confrontational. For instance, instead of saying, "You always ignore my suggestions," try saying, "I feel unheard when my suggestions are not considered." Framing your statements with "I" puts the focus on your feelings and experiences, making it easier for the other person to understand your viewpoint without feeling attacked.

4. Practice Non-Verbal Communication:

Non-verbal cues play a significant role in communication during difficult conversations. Pay attention to your body language, tone of voice, and facial expressions. Maintain an open posture, avoid crossing your arms or fidgeting, and use a calm and respectful tone. Non-verbal cues that convey openness and respect help create a safe space for the conversation to unfold.

Managing Emotions:

Emotions often escalate during difficult conversations, making them harder to navigate. Understanding your own emotions as well as recognizing the emotions of others is essential for effective communication. Here are some strategies to manage emotions during difficult conversations:

1. Take a Pause:

When emotions run high, it can be helpful to take a break from the conversation. Excuse yourself momentarily to gather your thoughts and calm your emotions. Breathing exercises, meditation, or engaging in a physical activity can help restore your emotional balance, allowing for a more productive conversation when you return.

2. Practice Emotional Regulation:

During a difficult conversation, emotions may fluctuate, and it is important to regulate and manage them effectively. Be aware of triggers that may evoke strong emotions and work on redirecting them towards productive conversation. Practice self-control, and if needed, express your emotions assertively and respectfully.

3. Focus on Solutions, Not Blame:

Difficult conversations often involve discussing perceived failures or mistakes. Instead of dwelling on the past and assigning blame, shift the focus towards finding solutions. Collaboratively brainstorm options and work toward a resolution that satisfies both parties' needs. Keeping a problem-solving mindset can help maintain a constructive atmosphere and minimize hostility.

Navigating difficult conversations requires skill, empathy, and understanding. By applying effective communication techniques, managing emotions, and fostering a problem-solving mindset, we can transform these challenging conversations into opportunities for growth and strengthened relationships. Remember, difficult conversations are an integral part of life, and by learning to navigate them with grace and compassion, we can overcome obstacles and foster better understanding and connection with others.

Preparing for Challenging Discussions

In this chapter, we will delve into the crucial aspect of preparing for challenging discussions. Whether you are engaging in a debate, negotiating a contract, or addressing a conflict in your personal relationships, these conversations can be emotionally charged and mentally demanding. By adequately preparing yourself, you can navigate these discussions with more confidence and increase your chances of achieving a more positive outcome. In this chapter, we will explore five essential steps to effectively prepare for challenging discussions, enabling you to approach them with clarity and composure.

Step 1: Define Your Objectives

When embarking on a challenging discussion, it is vital to establish clear objectives before engaging with the other person. Take the time to reflect on what you want to accomplish through this conversation. Do you seek to resolve a conflict, find a solution, or gain a better understanding of the other person's perspective? By defining your objectives, you set a clear direction for the conversation and avoid getting sidetracked by emotional impulses.

To define your objectives, consider the following questions:

- What outcome would make this discussion successful?

- What specific changes or resolutions would you like to see?

- How can you ensure that both parties are satisfied with the outcome?

By answering these questions, you can outline your goals and set realistic expectations for the upcoming discussion.

Step 2: Research and Gather Information

To effectively prepare for challenging discussions, it is crucial to gather as much information as possible beforehand. Comprehensive research will provide you with a deeper understanding of the topic or issue at hand, equipping you with the knowledge necessary to counter opposing arguments or negotiate successfully.

Begin by exploring various sources such as books, articles, and reputable websites to gain more insight into the subject matter. Look for potential data, case studies, or expert opinions that support your perspective or provide counterarguments you may need to address. This research not only strengthens your position but also shows that you have put in the effort to be well-informed.

Additionally, if you are engaging in a personal or professional conversation, gather any relevant background information about the other person involved. Understanding their values, experiences, and motivations can help you tailor your approach, fostering a more productive and empathetic discussion.

Step 3: Identify Potential Challenges and Emotional Triggers

Challenging discussions often evoke strong emotions in both parties involved. By identifying potential challenges and emotional triggers beforehand, you can mentally prepare yourself to stay calm and composed during the conversation.

Consider the different perspectives and potential arguments that the other person may present. Anticipating their viewpoints enables you to prepare strong counterarguments or find common ground. It is also helpful to think about potential emotional triggers either of you might have. This self-awareness allows you to manage your own emotions and respond empathetically rather than react impulsively.

To further enhance your preparation, consider embracing personal development techniques such as mindfulness or meditation. These practices can help you stay present in the conversation without getting overwhelmed by negative emotions.

Step 4: Plan Your Communication Strategy

Crafting a well-thought-out communication strategy is vital in navigating challenging discussions successfully. Consider the following key elements when planning your approach:

1. Timing: Choose a suitable time and place for the discussion to ensure privacy and minimize distractions.

2. Tone: Be mindful of your tone and avoid aggressive or confrontational language. Strive for assertive and respectful communication throughout the conversation.

3. Active Listening: Prepare yourself to actively listen to the other person's perspective or concerns. Demonstrate empathy and seek to understand their point of view.

4. Non-Verbal Communication: Pay attention to your body language and facial expressions, as they can significantly impact the conversation. Maintain open and welcoming gestures, encouraging an atmosphere of trust and collaboration.

5. Use "I" Statements: Frame your arguments or concerns using "I" statements rather than accusatory language. This approach fosters a non-confrontational environment and focuses on expressing your feelings or needs.

By planning your communication strategy in advance, you are more likely to facilitate a respectful and productive dialogue.

Step 5: Practice and Seek Feedback

Finally, prior to engaging in a challenging discussion, practice expressing your thoughts and arguments with a trusted confidant or mentor. Role-playing different scenarios can help you refine your communication skills and gain confidence in articulating your perspective effectively.

After each practice session, seek feedback from your practice partner. Ask them for their honest impressions of your communication style, strengths, and areas for improvement. Utilize this feedback to refine your approach and identify any blind spots that may hinder your success in the actual discussion.

Preparing for challenging discussions is an essential skill that can positively impact various aspects of our personal and professional lives. By defining objectives, conducting thorough research, identifying potential challenges, planning your communication strategy, and practicing with feedback, you can significantly enhance your ability to navigate these conversations effectively.

Remember, effective preparation increases your confidence, ensures a better understanding of the topic at hand, and enables the exploration of mutually beneficial outcomes. It is an investment in both your personal growth and the development of fruitful relationships in every area of your life.

Staying Calm under Pressure

Life is full of challenges, and at times, these challenges can lead us into high-pressure situations. Whether it's a demanding work environment, a crucial presentation, or a personal crisis, the ability to remain calm under pressure is a valuable skill that can significantly impact our success and well-being. This chapter explores the various aspects of staying calm under pressure, providing practical strategies and insights to help us navigate stressful situations with poise and composure.

Understanding the Impact of Pressure

To effectively manage pressure, it's essential to first understand its impact on our physical and mental well-being. When we find ourselves in high-stress situations, our bodies react through the release of stress hormones, such as cortisol and adrenaline. These hormones trigger the "fight or flight" response, preparing us to either face the challenge head-on or flee from it. While this response can be helpful in immediate danger, it can be detrimental when it becomes chronic or prolonged.

The consequences of prolonged exposure to pressure can be severe. People experiencing chronic stress may encounter a range of physical symptoms, including headaches, digestive issues, and weakened immune systems. Additionally, prolonged stress can have detrimental effects on our mental health, leading to anxiety, depression, and burnout.

Recognizing the Signs of Pressure

Before we can address how to stay calm under pressure, it's crucial to recognize the signs and symptoms of pressure. Each individual reacts differently to stress, so being attuned to our own physical, emotional, and behavioral responses is essential. Some common signs of pressure include:

1. Physical Symptoms: Increased heart rate, rapid breathing, tension headaches, muscle tightness, and digestive problems.

2. Emotional Symptoms: Irritability, anxiety, restlessness, mood swings, and feeling overwhelmed.

3. Behavioral Symptoms: Difficulty concentrating, decreased productivity, changes in eating or sleeping patterns, and increased reliance on unhealthy coping mechanisms, such as excessive alcohol or drug use.

By actively monitoring ourselves for these signs, we can take early action to mitigate their impacts and prevent an escalation of pressure.

Practical Strategies for Staying Calm under Pressure

While everyone faces pressure differently, there are several proven strategies that can help us stay calm and composed in stressful situations. Incorporating these techniques into our daily lives can build resilience and equip us with the skills necessary to tackle any challenge that comes our way.

1. Deep Breathing: Deep breathing exercises are simple yet powerful tools for calming the body and mind. When we feel pressure mounting, taking slow, deep breaths can activate the body's relaxation response, reducing heart rate and promoting a sense of calm. To practice deep breathing, find a quiet space, inhale deeply through your nose, hold the breath for a few seconds, and then exhale slowly through the mouth. Repeat this process for several minutes until you feel a sense of peace and equilibrium.

2. Mindfulness and Meditation: Mindfulness is the practice of intentionally focusing one's attention on the present moment, without judgment. By cultivating mindfulness, we develop the capacity to observe our thoughts and emotions objectively, reducing their power to control us. Regular meditation and mindfulness practices can train the brain to remain calm and centered, even in high-pressure situations. Experiment with various techniques such as guided meditation, body scans, or mindful walking to find what works best for you.

3. Positive Self-Talk: The way we talk to ourselves during stressful moments greatly influences our ability to remain calm. Negative self-talk can intensify pressure and increase anxiety levels. Counteract these effects by cultivating positive self-talk. Remind yourself of past successes, emphasize your strengths, and affirm your ability to handle challenges. By reframing your inner dialogue, you can shift your mindset from one of doubt to one of confidence.

4. Time Management and Prioritization: Often, feeling overwhelmed by pressure is a result of poor time management and an inability to effectively prioritize tasks. Learning to manage your time and identify which tasks are most critical not only helps alleviate stress but also increases efficiency and productivity. Break down larger projects into smaller, more manageable tasks, and create a schedule or to-do list that allows for realistic time allocations. By doing so, you'll gain a sense of control over your workload, reducing pressure and allowing for a focused approach.

5. Seeking Support and Building Connections: Navigating pressure alone can be challenging. Reach out to your support network, whether it consists of friends, family, mentors, or colleagues, and share your challenges and concerns. Talking through stressful situations with trusted individuals can provide valuable perspective, advice, and encouragement. Additionally, building supportive relationships at work can help create a conducive environment for handling pressure collectively.

The Importance of Self-Care

No discussion on staying calm under pressure would be complete without addressing the critical role that self-care plays in our overall well-being. Engaging in self-care activities boosts our resilience, equipping us with the tools necessary to cope with challenging situations effectively. Here are some key self-care practices to consider:

1. Physical Exercise: Regular exercise not only enhances physical health but also reduces stress, improves mood, and increases our overall resilience to pressure. Engage in activities that you enjoy, such as jogging, yoga, or dancing, and make them a regular part of your routine.

2. Healthy Lifestyle Choices: Proper nutrition, adequate sleep, and limited caffeine and alcohol intake are essential components of self-care. A well-nourished body and a rested mind are better equipped to handle stress.

3. Hobbies and Leisure Activities: Engaging in activities that bring joy and relaxation can provide a valuable outlet for stress. Dedicate time to hobbies, such as painting, playing an instrument, gardening, or reading, as these activities can serve as a form of mental escape from pressure.

4. Restorative Practices: Explore different restorative practices, such as taking warm baths, practicing aromatherapy, or listening to soothing music. These activities can trigger the body's relaxation response, alleviating stress and promoting a state of calm.

Learning to stay calm under pressure is a skill that can greatly enhance our lives both personally and professionally. By understanding the impact of pressure, recognizing its signs, and adopting practical strategies for maintaining composure, we can effectively navigate stressful situations with resilience and grace. Furthermore, prioritizing self-care ensures that we are equipped with the physical and mental well-being needed to face challenges head-on. So, take a deep breath, embrace these strategies, and seize the opportunities that pressure presents. Remember, staying calm under pressure is not about eliminating stress, but about mastering it and harnessing its power for personal growth and success.

Acknowledging Emotions

Emotions are an integral part of our human experience. They color our lives, influencing our thoughts, behaviors, and interactions with others. Yet, all too often, we overlook the significance of acknowledging and understanding our emotions, opting instead to suppress, ignore, or even deny them. In this chapter, we will delve into the importance of acknowledging emotions and explore various strategies and techniques for effectively embracing these powerful forces within ourselves.

The Nature of Emotions

Before we can fully understand the importance of acknowledging emotions, it is crucial to grasp the nature and purpose of these complex psychological experiences. Emotions represent our instinctive responses to internal and external stimuli, providing us with valuable cues about our needs, desires, and overall well-being. They are deeply intertwined with our thoughts, memories, and bodily sensations, creating a holistic experience unique to each individual.

Emotions serve as messengers, delivering vital information about our internal states. For example, the experience of fear alerts us to potential danger, prompting us to take precautionary measures.

Happiness, on the other hand, signals contentment and fulfillment, a reflection of our overall positive well-being. Each emotion carries specific meanings and serves distinct purposes, making it essential to acknowledge and validate them rather than dismissing or ignoring their existence.

The Dangers of Neglecting Emotions

It is not uncommon for individuals to suppress or avoid their emotions, believing that such actions will lead to greater emotional stability and control. However, neglecting our emotions can have severe consequences on our mental and physical health. When emotions go unacknowledged, they tend to bottle up, intensify, and manifest in unexpected ways—often resulting in high levels of stress, anxiety, depression, or even physical ailments.

Moreover, suppressed emotions can wreak havoc on our relationships and overall well-being. Unresolved emotional wounds may resurface inappropriately, leading to outbursts, damaging conflicts, or even a total breakdown in communication. By acknowledging our emotions promptly, we can address their underlying causes and thereby prevent further complications.

Strategies for Acknowledging Emotions

Now that we understand the value of acknowledging emotions, let us explore various strategies and techniques that can help us engage with our emotional experiences effectively.

1. Cultivating Mindfulness: Mindfulness is a practice that involves fostering a non-judgmental awareness of the present moment. By learning to be fully present and attuned to our senses, we can observe and identify our emotions as they arise. Being mindful allows us to detach from our emotions temporarily and gain a greater understanding of their nature and impact on our overall well-being.

2. Journaling: Writing down our emotions in a journal can be a therapeutic way to acknowledge and process them. By putting our feelings into words, we give them tangible form, making it easier to reflect upon and gain insight into their origins and implications. Regular journaling can provide us with a comprehensive record of our emotional experiences, enabling us to identify patterns and triggers.

3. Seeking Emotional Support: Acknowledging and processing our emotions does not necessarily mean doing so in isolation. Reaching out to trusted friends, family members, or mental health professionals can offer valuable support and an external perspective. Engaging in open and honest conversations about our emotions can foster emotional resilience and growth.

4. Creativity and Expression: Engaging in creative outlets such as art, music, or dance can provide a powerful means of acknowledging and releasing emotions. Through creative expression, we can tap into our emotional core and channel our feelings in constructive ways. Artistic endeavors foster a safe and non-threatening space for us to explore and embrace our emotions without fear of judgment or consequences.

5. Self-Compassion: Compassion for oneself is an essential component of effectively acknowledging and understanding emotions. It involves treating ourselves with kindness, empathy, and understanding, especially in challenging or distressing situations. By cultivating self-compassion, we create a nurturing environment that encourages the honest recognition and acceptance of our emotions.

Emotions are an intrinsic part of being human—an intricate tapestry of experiences that enrich our lives. By acknowledging and understanding our emotions, we develop a greater self-awareness and enhance our emotional intelligence. Rather than resisting or avoiding them, we should instead embrace our emotions as valuable sources of information and guidance. Through mindful practices, journaling, seeking emotional support, creative expression, and self-compassion, we can discover the transformative power of acknowledging our emotions. By doing so, we open ourselves to a more profound understanding of ourselves, our relationships, and our world.

Finding Compromise

In the realm of human interaction, compromise is an essential skill for navigating the complexities of relationships and achieving mutual understanding. Whether it is in personal relationships, workplace dynamics, or negotiations between nations, the ability to find common ground and strike a balance is pivotal for harmony and progress. In this chapter, we explore the art of compromise, examining the various factors that influence our ability to compromise and offering practical strategies to overcome obstacles and reach mutually beneficial solutions.

Understanding Compromise:

Compromise is often mistakenly perceived as a sign of weakness or surrender, but in reality, it is an integral part of healthy communication and problem-solving. At its core, compromise involves each party involved giving up or modifying their initial positions in the pursuit of arriving at a middle ground that satisfies the interests of all parties involved.

In many instances, compromise is crucial because it promotes effective collaboration, fosters trust and empathy, and paves the way for sustainable long-term solutions. However, compromise can also be challenging, as conflicting interests, pride, and a lack of effective communication can hinder the process. Therefore, it is essential to develop the necessary skills to navigate through these challenges and find compromise.

Obstacles to Compromise:

Compromise may seem straightforward in theory, but in practice, various obstacles can undermine the process. One primary obstacle is a lack of open-mindedness, where individuals hold rigid and unwavering positions, refusing to consider alternative perspectives and potential solutions. This closed-mindedness can stem from factors like personal biases, cultural or societal pressures, or past experiences that have shaped an individual's mindset.

Another obstacle is the fear of giving in or losing ground. When individuals approach compromise from a competitive mindset, they often prioritize their own interests over finding common ground. This self-oriented approach can lead to a win-lose mentality, escalating conflicts, and impeding the possibility of finding a mutually beneficial solution.

Moreover, ineffective communication skills can hinder compromise by preventing the clear expression of needs, concerns, and interests. Misunderstandings can arise when parties fail to actively listen, express themselves clearly, and seek to understand the root causes of disagreements.

Strategies for Effective Compromise:

Overcoming obstacles and achieving successful compromise requires a combination of self-reflection, effective communication, and problem-solving techniques. Here are some strategies that can help facilitate the compromise process:

1. Develop Empathy and Active Listening Skills:

Empathy plays a crucial role in compromise, as it enables individuals to understand and appreciate the perspectives, needs, and concerns of others. By actively listening – truly understanding and engaging with what is being said – we can bridge the gap between opposing views and foster empathy. This active listening involves avoiding interruptions, asking clarifying questions, and showing genuine interest in understanding the motivations and emotions behind each position.

2. Separate Interests from Positions:

To find a viable compromise, it is essential to separate interests from positions. Interests represent the underlying needs, desires, or concerns that drive each party's position, while positions refer to the specific demands or solutions they propose. By focusing on identifying shared interests, which often lay beneath surface-level positions, individuals can find creative solutions that satisfy everybody involved.

3. Brainstorm and Encourage Creativity:

Brainstorming sessions provide a platform for generating innovative solutions. Encouraging creativity by exploring a wide range of possibilities, even seemingly outlandish ones, can lead to unexpected breakthroughs. By suspending judgment during the brainstorming phase, participants can freely express their ideas, fostering a collaborative environment that nurtures compromise.

4. Seek Mediation or Third-Party Involvement:

In situations where compromise proves elusive, seeking mediation or involving a neutral, unbiased third party can offer fresh perspectives and prevent conflicts from reaching a stalemate. A skilled mediator can facilitate productive conversations, ensure that all voices are heard, and guide parties towards mutually acceptable solutions.

5. Develop Effective Problem-Solving Skills:

When attempting compromise, it is vital to approach problem-solving with a solution-oriented mindset. This involves breaking complex issues down into manageable components and focusing on generating practical, actionable solutions. By adopting a problem-solving approach, individuals can prioritize the positive outcomes and shared objectives, rather than getting stuck in a cycle of blame or power struggle.

Finding compromise is a delicate balance that requires a willingness to understand, adapt, and communicate effectively. By recognizing the importance of compromise in various aspects of our lives and actively working towards it, we can foster healthier relationships, promote collaboration, and achieve sustainable solutions to complex problems. Embracing compromise as a valuable tool for growth and progress is a cornerstone of human interaction, contributing to a more harmonious and interconnected world.

Chapter 6: Assertiveness Across Different Contexts

Assertiveness is an essential skill that allows individuals to express their thoughts, feelings, and needs effectively while respecting the boundaries of others. It offers a healthy balance between passivity and aggression, enabling individuals to communicate their ideas confidently and assertively. However, assertiveness can manifest differently in various contexts, such as personal relationships, the workplace, and social settings. Understanding how to adapt and apply assertiveness across these contexts is crucial for achieving effective communication and maintaining healthy relationships. In this chapter, we will explore the concept of assertiveness in different contexts and learn strategies to develop and improve this valuable skill.

I. Assertiveness in Personal Relationships

Personal relationships form the foundation of our lives and are where assertiveness truly comes into play. Whether it's our family, close friends, or romantic partners, being able to express ourselves clearly and honestly is crucial for fostering positive relationships and resolving conflicts.

1. Communication in Intimate Relationships

Intimate relationships require a high degree of open and honest communication. However, striking the right balance between expressing our needs and listening to others' needs can be challenging. Assertiveness plays a significant role in maintaining healthy relationships by promoting effective communication, active listening, and empathy.

2. Conflict Resolution

Conflicts are inevitable in any relationship, but how we handle them can determine their impact on our relationships. Assertiveness allows us to express our feelings and needs without resorting to aggression or passive avoidance. By using "I" statements, active listening skills, and seeking compromise, we can resolve conflicts constructively and strengthen our personal relationships.

II. Assertiveness in the Workplace

Effective assertiveness is invaluable in the professional sphere as it can lead to increased productivity, improved teamwork, and enhanced job satisfaction. Applying assertiveness at work requires understanding the appropriate balance between being assertive and respectful in different situations.

1. Assertive Communication with Colleagues

Assertiveness is essential when working alongside colleagues to establish boundaries, share ideas, and address conflicts. By clearly expressing our thoughts and opinions, actively listening, and respectfully providing and receiving feedback, we create an environment conducive to cooperation and collaboration.

2. Assertive Leadership

Leaders who know how to assert themselves effectively inspire trust and respect from their teams. Assertive leaders communicate expectations clearly, give constructive feedback, and encourage open dialogue. By embracing assertiveness, leaders can create a positive work environment and promote the professional growth of their team members.

III. Assertiveness in Social Settings

Social situations often present unique challenges for assertiveness. Meeting new people, engaging in small talk, and navigating group dynamics all require a certain level of assertiveness to establish connections and express oneself authentically.

1. Assertiveness in Small Talk

Engaging in small talk can often feel trivial, but it plays a crucial role in establishing connections with others. Assertive small talk involves showing genuine interest, active listening, and expressing oneself confidently to create meaningful conversations and build relationships.

2. Assertiveness in Group Settings

Assertiveness within groups can be challenging, as various personalities and dynamics come into play. Being assertive in a group means finding a balance between voicing one's perspectives and respecting others' opinions. Active participation, effective communication, and diplomacy are key to successful assertiveness in group settings.

Developing assertiveness across different contexts is an ongoing process that requires self-awareness, practice, and adaptability. As we navigate personal relationships, the workplace, and social settings, honing our assertiveness skills allows us to express ourselves confidently, build healthier relationships, and achieve our goals effectively. By understanding the nuances of assertiveness in each context and employing appropriate strategies, we can cultivate assertiveness as a powerful tool for personal and professional growth.

Assertive Communication at Work

In any workplace, effective communication plays a vital role in building successful interpersonal relationships and promoting a positive work environment. Among the various communication styles, assertive communication stands out as a powerful tool that empowers individuals to express their thoughts, needs, and concerns while respecting others' boundaries. This chapter will delve into the concept of assertive communication at work, its benefits, and how it can be applied in various workplace scenarios.

Understanding Assertive Communication:
Assertive communication is a style of expression that combines confidence, clarity, and respect for oneself and others. It involves openly expressing thoughts, feelings, and needs in a manner that is direct, honest, and considerate. This communication style allows individuals to express themselves effectively while maintaining healthy working relationships.

Benefits of Assertive Communication at Work:
Implementing assertive communication in the workplace offers numerous advantages for both individuals and organizations. Here are some key benefits:

1. Improved Interpersonal Relationships:

Assertive communication fosters trust and mutual respect among colleagues. By clearly articulating their thoughts, individuals create a supportive environment where ideas can be freely discussed. This, in turn, strengthens collaboration and encourages teamwork.

2. Enhanced Problem-Solving:

Assertive communicators have a higher likelihood of resolving conflicts and addressing issues effectively. They can express their concerns without aggression or hostility and engage in open dialogues to find mutually beneficial solutions. This leads to a more harmonious work environment where challenges are met head-on and resolved efficiently.

3. Increased Self-Confidence:

Practicing assertive communication can boost an individual's self-esteem and self-confidence. When individuals feel empowered to express their opinions and assert their needs, they are more likely to take on new challenges, voice innovative ideas, and contribute actively to the growth and success of the organization.

4. Reduced Stress and Anxiety:

One of the significant advantages of assertive communication lies in its ability to reduce stress and anxiety levels at work. Assertive individuals feel less pressure to conform to others' expectations or engage in passive-aggressive behaviors. By expressing their concerns honestly and openly, they can avoid bottling up emotions, leading to a healthier work-life balance.

5. Clearer Communication:

The assertive style promotes clarity and accuracy in communication. Assertive individuals use precise language, maintaining an appropriate tone, and providing relevant details. This ensures that their message is conveyed accurately, reducing the chances of misinterpretation or misunderstandings among team members.

Applying Assertive Communication Techniques:

To effectively implement assertive communication in the workplace, individuals should practice various techniques suited to different scenarios. Let us explore a few common workplace scenarios and how assertive communication can be applied in each:

1. Giving Constructive Feedback:

Providing feedback is an essential part of fostering professional growth. When offering constructive criticism, it is important to be assertive, focusing on the behavior or action rather than attacking the individual. Begin by stating the specific behavior that needs attention, providing examples, and explaining its impact. Reiterate that the intention is to facilitate growth and improvement, while also highlighting the individual's positive attributes and contributions.

2. Dealing with Difficult Colleagues:

In any workplace, there may be instances where individuals encounter difficult colleagues who exhibit aggressive or passive-aggressive behavior. When faced with such circumstances, assertive communication can help maintain a respectful environment. Engage in open dialogues to address concerns, set boundaries firmly, and express how their behavior impacts teamwork and productivity. It is crucial to remain calm, composed, and focused on finding resolutions while avoiding personal attacks or blame games.

3. Negotiating Responsibilities:

In a collaborative work environment, negotiating responsibilities and workloads is crucial to maintain a fair distribution of tasks. Assertive individuals can negotiate effectively by clearly articulating their workload concerns, expressing their capabilities and limitations, and proposing alternative solutions that promote efficiency. This approach enables the team to come to agreements that work for everyone involved.

4. Setting Boundaries:

Setting boundaries is essential to maintain a healthy work-life balance and avoid becoming overwhelmed by excessive workload or unreasonable demands. Assertive communication empowers individuals to express their needs and limitations openly. Clearly state what you can and cannot commit to, suggest alternative solutions, and emphasize the importance of maintaining balance to ensure long-term performance and well-being.

5. Expressing Dissent or Disagreement:

In a workplace that encourages diverse perspectives, it is natural for individuals to have differences of opinion or disagreement. Assertive communication allows individuals to express dissent respectfully. Focus on the issue at hand, provide logical arguments supported by facts or data, and actively listen to others' perspectives. This approach facilitates constructive debates and encourages open-mindedness while promoting a culture of innovation and continuous improvement.

Assertive communication is an invaluable skill that can transform workplace dynamics and contribute to professional growth and success. By practicing assertive communication techniques, individuals can establish strong interpersonal relationships, improve problem-solving abilities, enhance self-confidence, and reduce stress and anxiety levels. The benefits of assertive communication extend beyond the individual, positively impacting the entire team and organization. Thus, investing time and effort into developing assertive communication skills is an investment in building productive and fulfilling professional relationships.

Assertiveness in Relationships

Assertiveness is a valuable skill to possess in any type of relationship, be it romantic, familial, or professional. It is a communication style that allows individuals to express their needs, opinions, and boundaries in a clear and respectful manner. In this chapter, we will explore the importance of assertiveness in relationships, its benefits, and how it can be cultivated to enhance the quality of our interactions with others.

Understanding Assertiveness:

Assertiveness lies on a continuum, with passive behavior on one extreme end, and aggressive behavior on the other. While passive individuals tend to avoid conflict and prioritize others' needs over their own, aggressive individuals often exhibit dominance and disregard for others' feelings. Assertiveness, however, strikes a balance between these two extremes, enabling individuals to express their thoughts, feelings, and needs without infringing upon the rights of others.

Benefits of Assertiveness in Relationships:

Practicing assertiveness in relationships can bring about numerous benefits, both for individuals and their connections with others.

Firstly, assertiveness fosters honest and open communication, allowing both parties to express themselves freely. This leads to a deeper understanding of one another's perspectives, promoting empathy and nurturing a stronger connection.

Moreover, assertiveness empowers individuals by enhancing their self-esteem and self-confidence. When one learns to assert their needs and boundaries, they gain a sense of control over their own lives and relationships. This self-assurance positively impacts various aspects of their life, including their mental well-being, decision-making abilities, and overall satisfaction.

Furthermore, assertiveness plays a crucial role in conflict resolution. By openly addressing differences and concerns, individuals can work towards finding mutually beneficial solutions. This not only strengthens the relationship but also helps avoid passive-aggressive behavior, resentment, and long-standing conflicts.

Developing Assertiveness:

While some individuals may naturally possess assertiveness, many others find it challenging to express themselves openly and honestly. The good news is that assertiveness can be developed and honed with practice. Here are some strategies to cultivate assertiveness in relationships:

1. Recognize and Validate Your Feelings:

The first step in becoming more assertive is to cultivate self-awareness. Acknowledge and understand your emotions, needs, and boundaries without judgment. When you validate your feelings, you are better equipped to express them assertively to others.

2. Practice Active Listening:

Effective communication lies not only in expressing oneself but also in actively listening to others. Develop your listening skills by giving your undivided attention, allowing the other person to speak without interruption, and demonstrating your understanding through appropriate verbal and non-verbal cues.

3. Use "I" Statements:

When communicating your needs or concerns, employing "I" statements can be highly effective. By stating your thoughts or emotions using "I" instead of "you," you take ownership of your feelings, thus avoiding blaming or accusing the other person. This not only prevents defensiveness but also encourages a more constructive dialogue.

4. Learn to Say No:

Setting boundaries and saying no when necessary is a crucial aspect of assertiveness. Recognize that it is impossible to please everyone at all times. Practice assertively declining requests or demands that are not aligned with your values, needs, or personal limits. Remember, saying no when needed does not make you selfish or uncaring; it signifies self-respect and autonomy.

5. Use Positive Body Language:

Non-verbal cues, such as body language, play a significant role in assertive communication. Maintain eye contact, use open and relaxed gestures, and adopt an upright posture to convey confidence and openness. Be mindful of your tone of voice, ensuring it is firm but respectful, avoiding passive or aggressive language.

6. Practice Empathy:

Assertiveness is not about disregarding the feelings or needs of others; rather, it involves active consideration and empathy towards their perspectives. Put yourself in the other person's shoes, listen attentively, and reflect their feelings to validate their experiences. This fosters an atmosphere of mutual understanding and respect.

7. Seek Support:

Developing assertiveness may feel challenging, especially if you have a history of passivity or struggle with self-esteem. Seek support from trusted friends, family members, or a therapist who can provide guidance, encouragement, and practical advice on assertive communication techniques.

Assertiveness is a skill worth cultivating in all aspects of our lives, particularly in relationships. By mastering assertive communication, we can create more genuine and fulfilling connections, resolve conflicts effectively, and strengthen our sense of self. Remember, developing assertiveness takes time, practice, and patience, but the rewards it brings to our relationships and personal growth are immeasurable.

Dealing with Aggressive Individuals

In our daily lives, we often encounter people who display aggressive behavior, whether it be in the workplace, at social events, or even within our own families. Dealing with aggressive individuals can be challenging and emotionally draining, but understanding how to handle such situations can greatly alleviate their impact on our overall well-being. This chapter aims to provide valuable insights and practical techniques for effectively dealing with aggressive individuals in a variety of contexts. By adopting these strategies, we can enhance our communication skills, diffuse tense situations, and promote a harmonious atmosphere.

Understanding Aggression:

Before delving into techniques for dealing with aggressive individuals, it is crucial to first comprehend the root causes and underlying factors of aggression. Aggression often stems from frustration, fear, insecurity, or feelings of inadequacy. Moreover, external factors such as stress, environmental triggers, or even past traumatic experiences can contribute to aggressive behavior. Recognizing these causes allows us to empathize with aggressive individuals and better address the root cause of their actions.

Active Listening:

One of the fundamental principles in dealing with aggressive individuals is actively listening to what they have to say. Being fully present in the moment and demonstrating genuine interest in the other person's perspective can go a long way in defusing a potentially aggressive situation. By listening attentively, we show respect and validate their feelings, which can help navigate them towards a more constructive and non-threatening dialogue.

Remaining Calm and Composed:

When faced with aggression, our natural instinct might urge us to respond aggressively in return or to become defensive. However, maintaining our composure and remaining calm is essential for diffusing the situation. Our emotions can be contagious, and by remaining calm, we prevent escalating the aggression further. Through our composed demeanor, we set the tone for a more constructive dialogue and encourage the aggressive individual to reciprocate with a calmer approach.

Avoiding Personal Attacks:

When dealing with an aggressive individual, it is important to focus on the issue or behavior at hand rather than attacking their character. Resorting to personal attacks fuels aggression and can quickly turn a disagreement into a full-blown conflict. Instead, express your concerns using "I" statements, as this emphasizes your perspective rather than making accusatory statements that can trigger defensiveness in the other person.

Maintaining Boundaries:

In some cases, aggressive individuals may attempt to encroach upon our personal boundaries, whether verbally or physically. It is imperative to establish and assert our personal boundaries firmly but respectfully. Clearly communicate what is acceptable and what is not while maintaining a non-confrontational attitude. By setting our boundaries, we safeguard our emotional well-being while also providing the aggressive individual with clear limitations for their behavior.

Empathy and Understanding:

Empathy is a powerful tool in dealing with aggressive individuals. By attempting to understand their perspective and showing empathy towards their emotions, we create an environment where they feel heard and acknowledged. When faced with aggression, try acknowledging their frustration, fear, or insecurities, as this can help calm their emotions and facilitate more open communication. Empathy allows for the possibility of finding common ground and shared solutions that can benefit both parties involved.

Using Assertive Communication:

Assertive communication is a crucial skill when dealing with aggressive individuals. This style of communication involves expressing your thoughts, feelings, and needs confidently and respectfully, without undermining or attacking the other person. By using "I" statements, maintaining eye contact, and adopting a firm yet composed tone, you convey your message effectively while respecting the rights and boundaries of the aggressive individual.

Defusing Tension:

During confrontations with aggressive individuals, tensions may run high, which could potentially escalate the situation further. To defuse tense situations, it can be helpful to suggest taking a short break or stepping back momentarily. This pause provides an opportunity for emotions to settle, allowing both parties to regain control and perspective. Engaging in deep breathing exercises or focusing on a calming thought can help ease heightened emotions.

Offering Solutions and Compromises:

When faced with aggression, focusing on finding solutions and compromises can be immensely valuable. Help the aggressive individual recognize that their concerns are being acknowledged by actively involving them in the problem-solving process. By jointly evaluating potential solutions, you empower them to take ownership and participate constructively in finding a resolution that meets both parties' needs.

Seeking External Support:

In cases where aggression persists or becomes physically threatening, it is essential to prioritize personal safety. Seeking external support, such as security personnel or law enforcement, can be necessary to diffuse such situations and ensure the safety of all involved parties. Remember, your well-being and safety are paramount, and involving external support is a measure of prudence and responsibility.

Dealing with aggressive individuals is a challenging endeavor that requires patience, empathy, and effective communication skills. By understanding the underlying causes of aggression, actively listening, remaining calm, and employing assertive communication techniques, we can navigate aggressive encounters with more ease and confidence. While these strategies may not guarantee immediate resolution, they provide a foundation for promoting healthier and more constructive interactions. Remember, practice makes perfect, so keep honing your skills in dealing with aggression, and you will find yourself better equipped to handle such situations gracefully.

Assertiveness in Public Speaking

Public speaking is a unique art that combines effective communication, confidence, and assertiveness. While many may assume that assertiveness is synonymous with arrogance or aggressiveness, in the context of public speaking, it plays a crucial role in conveying your message effectively and persuasively to your audience. This chapter delves deep into the concept of assertiveness in public speaking, exploring its meaning, importance, and how one can develop assertiveness skills to become a more impactful public speaker.

Understanding Assertiveness:

Before we dive into the realm of public speaking, let us first grasp the concept of assertiveness. Assertiveness is a communication style characterized by the ability to express one's thoughts, beliefs, and needs with confidence and clarity while respecting the rights and opinions of others. It is a middle ground between passivity and aggression, allowing speakers to strike a fine balance when presenting their ideas.

Importance of Assertiveness in Public Speaking:

Assertiveness plays a pivotal role in public speaking, as it enables speakers to effectively engage their audience, establish credibility, and persuade them to adopt their viewpoints. Without assertiveness, speakers may come across as timid, hesitant, or uncertain, diminishing their impact and leaving the audience disinterested or skeptical. On the other hand, an overly aggressive approach may alienate the audience, leading to resistance or hostility. Therefore, assertiveness is the key to striking the right balance and capturing the attention and interest of the listeners.

Developing Assertiveness Skills:

Like any other skill, assertiveness can be developed and honed over time. Here are some techniques to help you enhance your assertiveness as a public speaker:

1. Building Self-Confidence:

Assertiveness stems from confidence, so it is crucial to work on strengthening your self-assurance. Practice positive self-talk, acknowledge your strengths, and build a strong belief in the value of your message. This will not only boost your confidence but also serve as a foundation for assertiveness in your speech.

2. Mastering Body Language:

Non-verbal cues play a significant role in conveying assertiveness. Maintain strong posture, make eye contact with the audience, and avoid excessive fidgeting or nervous gestures. These body language techniques will project confidence and assurance, making your speech more persuasive.

3. Speaking Clearly and Directly:

Assertive speakers are known for their clarity and directness in conveying their message. Work on articulating your thoughts concisely, using appropriate language, and avoiding any vague or ambiguous statements. Practice the art of being succinct while maintaining the impact and persuasiveness of your speech.

4. Active Listening:

Assertiveness is not just about conveying your thoughts but also actively listening to others' opinions. Acknowledge your audience, respond empathetically to their concerns, and incorporate their perspectives to establish a sense of inclusiveness. Engage in active listening to create a constructive dialogue, rather than a one-sided monologue.

5. Handling Questions and Challenges:

In public speaking, assertiveness manifests when addressing questions or challenges confidently and respectfully. Prepare yourself to encounter opposing viewpoints, and respond assertively by providing well-reasoned answers. Acknowledge differing opinions while expressing the validity of your own arguments, creating an environment of open discussion and debate.

6. Embracing Feedback:

Feedback is a valuable tool for self-improvement. Actively seek feedback from trusted mentors or colleagues to gain insights into your delivery, content, and overall assertiveness. Embrace constructive criticism and incorporate suggestions to refine your public speaking skills further.

Case Studies: Exemplary Assertive Speakers:
To illustrate the impact of assertiveness in public speaking, let us explore two exemplary speakers known for their assertive communication style.
1. Martin Luther King Jr. - Dr. King's assertiveness was a defining characteristic of his powerful speeches during the Civil Rights Movement. Through his crisp articulation and unwavering conviction, he mobilized masses, compelling them to challenge racial inequality and fight for justice.
2. Sheryl Sandberg - As a prominent business executive and author, Sandberg exudes assertiveness in her public speaking engagements. Her ability to command attention, express her views, and engage the audience has made her an influential voice on gender equality and women empowerment.
Assertiveness is an indispensable skill for public speakers aiming to make a lasting impact on their audience. By adopting the techniques mentioned above and studying the exemplary speakers, one can cultivate assertiveness, enhancing their ability to deliver persuasive and influential speeches. Remember, assertiveness is not about overpowering others but rather about conveying your message confidently, respectfully, and persuasively, while making space for collaborative dialogue and diverse viewpoints.

Chapter 7: Continuing Growth and Improvement

In the journey of life, growth and improvement are essential elements for personal development and success. It is through an ongoing commitment to expanding our knowledge, honing our skills, and cultivating our inner strengths that we can truly thrive and make a positive impact on the world around us. Chapter 8 of this book is dedicated to exploring the power of continued growth and improvement, delving into various aspects that contribute to our holistic development.

The Cycle of Growth and Improvement:

Before delving into the specific areas of growth and improvement, it is crucial to understand the inherent nature of the cycle itself. Growth and improvement should be viewed as an ongoing process, rather than a destination to be reached. It is a continuous journey characterized by constant learning, implementation, adaptation, and reflection. Embracing this cycle helps us develop resilience, adaptability, and an open mindset necessary for personal and professional growth.

Learning and Expanding Knowledge:

One of the key pillars of continued growth and improvement is a commitment to lifelong learning. In today's fast-paced world, where information is readily available, it becomes even more critical for us to stay curious, proactive, and constantly seek new knowledge. Cultivating a love for learning can be achieved through various means, such as reading books, attending seminars, taking online courses, or engaging in meaningful discussions with experts in our fields of interest. By continuously expanding our knowledge base, we equip ourselves with the necessary skills and insights to adapt to the evolving demands of the world around us.

Skill Development:

Alongside knowledge acquisition, honing our skills is crucial for growth and improvement. Skills can be acquired through deliberate practice, repetition, and consistent effort. Whether it be in areas of communication, problem-solving, leadership, creativity, or technical expertise, investing time and energy into skill development allows us to navigate challenges with ease and contribute meaningfully to our chosen endeavors. It is important to identify areas for improvement and set clear goals for skill enhancement, taking small steps towards mastery each day.

Embracing Failure and Taking Risks:

In the pursuit of growth and improvement, failure is not only inevitable but becomes a valuable stepping stone on our path to success. It is through adversity and setbacks that we learn the most invaluable lessons. By embracing failure as a necessary part of the process, we can develop resilience, adaptability, and a growth mindset. Alongside failure comes the need to take calculated risks, stepping outside our comfort zones to explore new possibilities. It is in these uncharted territories that we often find the greatest opportunities for growth and transformation.

Personal Well-being and Mindfulness:

As we strive for continued growth and improvement, it is crucial not to neglect our personal well-being. True growth encompasses more than just our professional lives; it involves nurturing our physical, mental, and emotional selves. Incorporating self-care practices into our daily routines, such as regular exercise, proper nutrition, adequate rest, and mindfulness activities, helps maintain a healthy balance and promotes holistic growth. By prioritizing our own well-being, we enhance our ability to thrive and have a positive impact on others and the world at large.

Continuous Self-Reflection:

Reflection plays a vital role in growth and improvement. Only through deep introspection can we truly understand our strengths, weaknesses, and areas for improvement. Regularly setting aside time for self-reflection allows us to evaluate our progress, track our achievements, and identify areas where growth is still needed. It helps us stay focused and aligned with our long-term objectives, while also fostering self-awareness and a willingness to adapt our strategies when necessary.

Seeking Feedback and Mentors:

No one can achieve true growth and improvement in isolation. Seeking feedback from others, especially those with more experience or expertise in our chosen fields, can provide invaluable insights and guidance. Constructive feedback allows us to uncover blind spots, refine our approaches, and accelerate our progress. Establishing relationships with mentors or role models can also greatly enhance our growth. Their wisdom and support can provide us with the motivation, knowledge, and encouragement needed to overcome challenges and unlock our full potential.

Contributing to Others:

Acknowledging the interconnected nature of growth, improvement, and fulfillment, it is important to recognize that our own growth journey should not solely be self-centered. By contributing to the growth and improvement of others, we create a ripple effect of positive change. Sharing our knowledge, offering support, and inspiring those around us helps create a supportive community, fostering an environment in which everyone thrives. Through meaningful connections and collaboration, we can collectively elevate ourselves and pave the way for a brighter future.

Chapter 8 has explored the key elements of continued growth and improvement on our journey towards personal and professional development. By embracing the cycle of learning, skill development, embracing failure and taking risks, prioritizing personal well-being, engaging in self-reflection, seeking feedback and mentors, and contributing to others, we can continue to grow and make a positive impact on the world. Remember, growth is a lifelong journey, and each day presents new opportunities for improvement. The true essence of growth lies in our commitment to adapt, learn, and evolve continuously.

Seeking Feedback

In our journey towards personal and professional growth, seeking feedback plays a pivotal role. Feedback serves as a powerful tool for self-improvement, allowing us to gain valuable insights into our strengths, weaknesses, and areas for development. It provides us with an external perspective that can bring about positive change and enhance our overall performance. As we delve into the art of seeking feedback, let us explore the various aspects of this practice and discover how it can shape our path to success.

Understanding the Importance of Feedback:

Feedback is an essential element of human communication. From infancy, we rely on feedback to learn and develop as individuals. It helps us understand the consequences of our actions, and through constant feedback, we refine our skills and make informed decisions. In our personal and professional lives, feedback functions in a similar way. It offers us a reality check and guides us towards better versions of ourselves.

Feedback fosters growth:

Feedback acts as a catalyst for personal and professional growth. By actively seeking feedback, we create opportunities for improvement and expand our potential. By being open to constructive criticism, we can identify areas where we may be falling short or ways in which we can enhance our skills. This willingness to learn and grow allows us to rise above mediocrity and strive for excellence.

Feedback enhances self-awareness:

Seeking feedback helps us in becoming more self-aware. Oftentimes, we may not fully recognize our strengths or acknowledge our weaknesses. Feedback from others provides us with a clearer picture of our abilities and limitations. It enables us to gain a better understanding of who we are, how we are perceived by others, and how our actions impact those around us. This self-awareness lays the foundation for personal and professional development.

The Art of Seeking Feedback:

While feedback is valuable, the manner in which we seek it can greatly influence its effectiveness. Here are some key considerations to keep in mind when seeking feedback:

1. Be open-minded and receptive:

To benefit from feedback, it is crucial to approach it with an open mind. Be willing to listen to alternative perspectives and embrace diverse opinions. Do not let defensiveness hinder your growth.

Remember, feedback is not a personal attack but an opportunity to grow and improve.

2. Seek input from diverse sources:

To gain a well-rounded understanding of your performance, seek feedback from a variety of sources. This could include mentors, colleagues, subordinates, friends, and family. Each person brings a unique perspective, allowing you to gather a comprehensive view of your strengths and areas for development. Embrace the diversity of opinions and insights that others can offer.

3. Ask specific and targeted questions:

When seeking feedback, it is important to ask specific and targeted questions. Instead of asking generic questions like, "How am I doing?" or "What do you think of my work?", ask more focused questions such as, "What areas do you think I can improve upon?" or "How would you suggest I enhance my communication skills?" Providing a clear context and seeking feedback on specific aspects will yield more valuable insights.

4. Create a safe and supportive environment:

To encourage others to provide honest feedback, it is crucial to create a safe and supportive environment. Assure them that their input is valued and that their opinions will be respected. Avoid becoming defensive or dismissive of feedback, as it may discourage others from sharing their thoughts in the future. Cultivate an environment where constructive criticism is welcomed and appreciated.

5. Reflect and act upon feedback:

Seeking feedback should not be a one-time event; it should be an ongoing process. After receiving feedback, take the time to reflect on the insights provided. Assess the clarity, accuracy, and relevance of the feedback and identify areas for improvement. Use this information to set actionable goals and develop strategies for growth. Feedback without action is merely information; it is in its implementation that it becomes transformational.

Seeking feedback is an integral part of our journey towards personal and professional growth. It enables us to gain a better understanding of ourselves, refine our skills, and strive for excellence. By approaching feedback with an open mind, seeking input from diverse sources, asking targeted questions, creating a supportive environment, and reflecting upon the feedback received, we can leverage this powerful tool to unlock our true potential. Embrace the art of seeking feedback and watch as it transforms you into a better version of yourself, propelling you towards success and fulfillment.

Learning from Role Models

Throughout our lives, we encounter various individuals who inspire and motivate us to become better versions of ourselves. These people, often referred to as role models, serve as beacons of light, guiding us down a path of personal growth and success. In this chapter, we will explore the concept of learning from role models, understanding the benefits they offer, and how we can integrate their teachings into our lives. Whether we admire a historical figure, a celebrity, or a family member, harnessing the power of role models can have a profound impact on our journey towards self-improvement.

Identifying Role Models:

One of the first steps in learning from role models is to identify those individuals who epitomize the qualities and traits we aspire to embody. Role models can come from various walks of life – they can be scientists, artists, athletes, or even close friends and family members. They often possess attributes that resonate with our personal values and goals, making it easier for us to connect with and learn from them.

When finding role models, it is crucial to consider their accomplishments, character, and how their actions align with our own principles. For instance, if we admire someone for their philanthropy, it is essential to analyze the reasons behind their charitable endeavors, looking for sincerity and a genuine desire to make a positive impact. By critically evaluating potential role models, we can ensure that the lessons we learn from them align with our personal growth objectives.

Learning through Observation:

Once we have identified role models, the next step is to observe and learn from their actions and behaviors. By paying attention to their approach to life, we can gain insights into how they have achieved success and personal fulfillment. Observing role models allows us to explore their decision-making processes, problem-solving techniques, and methods for overcoming obstacles. It is through witnessing their journeys that we can learn how to navigate our own.

Role models also offer us a unique opportunity to learn from their mistakes. By observing how they handle setbacks and failures, we gain invaluable lessons on resilience and perseverance. This knowledge is instrumental in equipping us with the mindset necessary to face our challenges with determination and optimism.

Emulating Positive Traits:

While it is essential to admire and learn from role models, we must also remember to maintain our authenticity. While we can strive to emulate positive traits of our role models, it is crucial not to lose sight of our individuality. Rather than trying to become a mere replica of our role models, we should focus on integrating the qualities that resonate with us into our own lives.

For example, if we admire a leader for their decisiveness and ability to inspire others, we can aim to develop those qualities within ourselves. By studying how they communicate and motivate, we can start to incorporate similar techniques into our interactions with others. However, it is vital to blend these traits with our unique personality and style, ensuring that we remain true to ourselves throughout the learning process.

Seeking Mentorship:

In some cases, individuals may have the opportunity to establish a direct mentor-mentee relationship with their role models, which can greatly enhance the learning experience. Seeking mentorship allows for more personalized guidance and support, enabling us to delve deeper into understanding our role models' mindset and achievements.

When approaching a potential mentor, it is essential to demonstrate genuine interest, commitment, and a willingness to learn. By respecting their time and expertise, we increase the likelihood of establishing and maintaining a mutually beneficial relationship.

Mentors can provide invaluable insights, advice, and accountability, accelerating our personal growth journey.

Role Models Inspiring Change:

Apart from individual growth, role models can inspire collective change by demonstrating what is possible and motivating groups of people towards a common cause. Throughout history, countless charismatic leaders have emerged, inspiring movements and initiating social transformations. These role models offer hope, ignite passion, and unite individuals from diverse backgrounds under a shared vision for a better future.

Whether it is a civil rights activist advocating for equality, an environmentalist working towards sustainability, or a social entrepreneur pioneering innovative solutions, role models offer inspiration to those seeking to make a difference. By learning from their approaches, we can become catalysts for change in our own communities, amplifying the impact of their teachings and spreading positive values to a wider audience.

Learning from role models is a powerful tool for personal and societal growth. By identifying and studying the individuals who embody the qualities and achievements we value, we can learn invaluable lessons from their journeys. Through observation, emulation, mentorship, and the collective inspiration they provide, role models act as guides, helping us navigate the complexities of life, strive for excellence, and make a positive impact on the world around us.

Practicing Empathy

In today's fast-paced world, it is easy to get caught up in our own lives, often forgetting about the experiences, emotions, and struggles of those around us. However, empathy is a fundamental skill that allows us to connect with others on a deeper level, understand their perspectives, and provide genuine support. In this chapter, we will explore the concept of empathy, its significance in our personal and professional lives, and various practices that can help us become more empathetic individuals.

Understanding Empathy:

Empathy is the ability to recognize, understand, and share the feelings of others. It goes beyond sympathy, which refers to feeling compassion for someone's pain or situation without necessarily understanding it. Empathy requires us to put ourselves in someone else's shoes, acknowledging their emotions without judgment and responding with genuine care and concern.

Why Practicing Empathy Matters:

Empathy plays a crucial role in building healthy relationships, fostering understanding, and promoting effective communication. When we are empathetic, we become more attuned to the needs and feelings of those around us, creating an environment of trust, respect, and support. Whether it's within our families, friendships, or professional relationships, empathy allows us to connect authentically and develop stronger bonds.

Benefits of Empathy in Personal Relationships:

In personal relationships, empathy helps create harmony and deepens emotional connections. When we genuinely understand and empathize with our loved ones, we can offer them the support and comfort they need during challenging times. By listening attentively and validating their feelings, we can strengthen our relationships, demonstrating that we are invested in their well-being and happiness.

Furthermore, empathy encourages open and honest communication, as it fosters an environment where individuals feel safe sharing their vulnerabilities and concerns. This leads to greater emotional intimacy, allowing couples, friends, and families to navigate conflicts more effectively and find mutually satisfying resolutions.

Benefits of Empathy in Professional Settings:

Empathy is not limited to personal relationships; it is equally important in professional settings. When we practice empathy in the workplace, we enhance our abilities to collaborate, inspire, and lead.

By understanding our colleagues' perspectives and experiences, we can better manage conflicts, solve problems, and promote teamwork.

Additionally, empathy enhances our leadership skills since it allows managers to recognize and respond to the needs of their team members effectively. By understanding their employees' challenges and aspirations, leaders can provide tailored guidance and support, fostering personal growth and professional development.

Practices for Cultivating Empathy:

1. Active Listening:

Active listening is a crucial practice for fostering empathy. It involves fully engaging with the speaker, paying attention to their verbal and non-verbal cues, and withholding judgment. By giving our undivided attention, maintaining eye contact, and providing verbal affirmations, we show that we genuinely care about the other person's feelings and experiences.

2. Perspective-Taking:

Perspective-taking involves actively trying to understand a situation from the other person's point of view. It requires temporarily setting aside our own assumptions, biases, and beliefs and stepping into their shoes. By considering the context, emotions, and background of others, we gain a deeper understanding of their experiences, allowing us to respond in a more compassionate and supportive manner.

3. Emotional Awareness:

Emotional awareness involves recognizing and acknowledging our own emotions and those of others. By developing emotional intelligence, we become more attuned to subtle cues, such as facial expressions, tone of voice, and body language. This heightened awareness enables us to respond appropriately to others' emotions, demonstrating empathy and creating a safe space for open communication.

4. Mindfulness:

Practicing mindfulness helps us become more present in the moment, enabling us to focus our attention on others instead of being preoccupied with our own thoughts. When we are fully present, we can listen more effectively, respond empathetically, and provide genuine support. Mindfulness also helps cultivate self-compassion, which is necessary for empathizing with others without feeling overwhelmed or emotionally drained.

5. Asking Open-Ended Questions:

Asking open-ended questions encourages meaningful conversations and fosters empathy. By asking questions that begin with "how," "what," or "why," we invite others to express themselves more deeply, allowing us to gain a better understanding of their experiences, thoughts, and emotions. Open-ended questions encourage individuals to reflect on their feelings, enhancing their own self-awareness, while also signaling that we are interested in their well-being.

6. Practicing Empathetic Language:

Using empathetic language involves choosing our words carefully to communicate understanding and compassion. Instead of immediately offering solutions or advice, we can acknowledge the other person's feelings and experiences by saying phrases like, "I can imagine how challenging that must be for you" or "It sounds like you're going through a difficult time." Empathetic language validates the other person's emotions and demonstrates our empathy and support.

Practicing empathy is a lifelong journey that requires continuous effort and self-reflection. By developing our empathetic skills, we can enrich our personal relationships, create more fulfilling professional interactions, and contribute to a more compassionate and understanding society. Remember, empathy is a powerful tool that has the potential to transform not only our lives but also the lives of those around us. Let us strive to cultivate empathy in our daily lives, making the world a more empathetic and supportive place for all.

Embracing Lifelong Learning

In today's rapidly evolving world, the pursuit of knowledge and personal development has taken on a new level of importance. Gone are the days when education was seen as something to be completed within the confines of a classroom or only during the early stages of life. Recognizing the value of continuous learning, many individuals are now embracing the concept of lifelong learning. In this chapter, we will delve into the various aspects of lifelong learning, exploring its benefits, challenges, and strategies for effectively incorporating it into our lives.

The Essence of Lifelong Learning:

Lifelong learning refers to the process of acquiring knowledge, skills, and insights throughout one's entire life. It is a holistic approach to personal growth that extends beyond formal education and encompasses both formal and informal learning experiences. The core principle behind lifelong learning is the recognition that education is not limited to a specific time period or institutional framework – it is a never-ending journey that can be undertaken at any age and in any context.

Benefits of Lifelong Learning:

1. Adaptation to Change: In a fast-paced and ever-changing world, the ability to adapt is crucial. Lifelong learning equips individuals with the skills and knowledge necessary to navigate through uncertainties and embrace change. By continuously building new competencies and staying up-to-date with emerging trends, individuals can remain relevant and adaptable in their personal and professional lives.

2. Personal Growth and Fulfillment: Lifelong learning fosters a sense of personal growth and fulfillment. Engaging in challenging intellectual pursuits not only stimulates the mind but also enhances confidence and self-esteem. It allows individuals to identify and pursue their passions, hobbies, and interests, leading to a more fulfilling and well-rounded life.

3. Career Advancement: In today's competitive job market, continuous learning is essential for career progression. Lifelong learners are better equipped to seize new opportunities, take on diverse roles, and demonstrate their willingness to adapt to changing job requirements. By expanding their skill set and knowledge base, individuals can enhance their employability and increase their chances of career advancement.

4. Cognitive Function and Well-being: Engaging in intellectual

activities has been linked to improved cognitive function and overall well-being. Lifelong learning challenges the mind, promotes critical thinking, and enhances problem-solving abilities. Studies have shown that keeping the brain active through learning can reduce the risk of cognitive decline, enhance memory, and improve mental health.

5. Social Connection and Networking: Lifelong learning can foster social connections and networking opportunities. Joining learning communities, attending workshops, and participating in educational programs provide avenues for individuals to meet like-minded individuals and expand their social circles. These connections can lead to collaboration, mentorship, and the sharing of ideas and experiences, thereby enriching the learning journey.

Challenges of Lifelong Learning:

While the benefits of lifelong learning are numerous, there are certain challenges that individuals may encounter along the way. These challenges include:

1. Time Constraints: Balancing work, family, and personal commitments can make it challenging to allocate time for learning. Lifelong learners need to effectively manage their time, prioritize their learning goals, and incorporate dedicated learning periods into their daily or weekly routines.

2. Financial Considerations: Some learning opportunities may come with associated costs, such as tuition fees, course materials, or travel expenses. Individuals must evaluate the financial implications of their learning choices and explore alternative options such as scholarships, online resources, and community programs.

3. Motivation and Discipline: Sustaining motivation and discipline over an extended period can be difficult. Without the structure and deadlines imposed by formal education, lifelong learners must rely on self-motivation and self-discipline to stay committed to their learning journey. Setting clear goals, tracking progress, and celebrating achievements can help maintain momentum and drive.

4. Overcoming Fear and Resistance to Change: Trying new things and stepping out of one's comfort zone can be intimidating. Lifelong learners must confront their fears and embrace the uncertainty that comes with acquiring new knowledge and skills. By adopting a growth mindset and viewing challenges as opportunities for growth, individuals can overcome resistance to change and embrace lifelong learning more effectively.

Strategies for Embracing Lifelong Learning:

1. Set Clear Goals: Determine your learning objectives, whether they are related to personal interests, career development, or specific skills. Setting clear goals will help you stay focused and motivated

throughout your learning journey.

2. Develop a Learning Plan: Create a learning plan that outlines the resources, materials, and activities you will engage in to meet your goals. This plan could include enrolling in courses, attending workshops, reading books, joining online communities, or participating in informal learning experiences.

3. Establish a Routine: Incorporate learning into your daily or weekly routine. Allocate dedicated time for learning, whether it's early mornings, evenings, weekends, or during lunch breaks. Consistency is key to maintaining momentum.

4. Embrace Technology and Online Learning: Leverage the power of technology and online platforms to access a vast array of learning resources. Online courses, webinars, podcasts, and educational websites offer flexible and accessible learning opportunities tailored to individual needs.

5. Create a Supportive Environment: Surround yourself with like-minded individuals who prioritize learning. Join learning communities, seek out mentors, or form study groups. Engaging with others who share similar interests will provide support, encouragement, and collaborative opportunities.

6. Reflect and Apply Learning: Reflect on what you have learned and

find opportunities to apply your knowledge and skills in real-life situations. Applying what you have learned reinforces the learning process and deepens your understanding.

7. Embrace Failure and Iteration: Remember that learning is a journey, and setbacks are inevitable. Embrace failure as a valuable learning experience and use it to refine your approach. By iterating and adapting, you will continually improve and grow.

8. Stay Curious: Cultivate a curious mindset and remain open to new ideas and perspectives. Embrace curiosity as a driving force for learning and seek out opportunities to explore diverse topics and disciplines.

Embracing lifelong learning is a mindset and a commitment to personal growth and development. It encourages individuals to view learning as a lifelong journey rather than a destination. By recognizing the many benefits, understanding the challenges, and implementing effective strategies, individuals can unlock the transformative power of lifelong learning. It is through this continuous pursuit of knowledge and personal growth that we can navigate the complexities of the modern world, adapt to change, and lead fulfilling lives.